HOMESPUN CURRICULUM

A Developmentally Appropriate Activities Guide

By Denise Theobald

Humanics Learning
P.O. Box 7400
Atlanta, GA 30357

HUMANICS
LEARNING

P.O. Box 7400
Atlanta, GA 30357

Full-page Illustrations and Graphic Design by Denise Theobald
All Other Illustrations by Suzi Howard
Cover Design by Jackie Kerr
Edited by Nancy Brand

First Printing 1998
Copyright 1998 Humanics Limited

Printed in the United States of America

Library of Congress Cataloging-in-Publication Data

Theobald, Denise S., 1953-
        Homespun Curriculum: A Developmentally Appropriate Activities Guide.
1.Toddlers—United States. 2. Day care centers—United States—Activity programs.
3.Education, Preschool—United States—Activity Programs.

ISBN: 0-89334-258-0

Preface

Homespun Curriculum has been written with many purposes in mind. It is a guide for parents who desire to become more involved in their children's development and learning, while spending quality time with them in the process. It is also intended to aid child care providers who want to give more to the children in their care and increase the quality of their profession. For the parents, providers, and early childhood education professionals who just want additional ideas or quick references, this information will expand their own creative resources.

A wide range of activities is presented in numerous educational and developmental areas. Most activities note skills. It is more difficult to plan projects with children when there is a wide range of ages, developmental stages, and capabilities. Therefore, one purpose of this home spun curriculum guide is to help modify activities in order to integrate the needs of different skill levels. With toddlers, preschoolers/kindergartners, and school age children, it is not always necessary to create three different projects. Just changing one basic project to meet the needs of all three groups will enable you to accomplish so much more, and all at the same time.

The majority of these activities is based upon the preschool/kindergarten child and give alternatives for toddlers, infants, and school age children (note: I have refrained from indicating specific ages because experience shows that comprehension, development, and skill levels do not always coincide with age level). Many activities are already appropriate for all different age groups and are not coded with an age differentiation.

A well-rounded foundation is the primary reason for including pre-educational activities in this curriculum. Kindergarten used to be entirely geared towards play and social adjustment, but today, children need to be more prepared educationally before starting school. Parents and providers can help them start preparing right from infancy and continue stimulating and teaching them throughout their youth. Remember, never underestimate a child's ability to learn and, at the same time, know the child's limitations to avoid frustration. Experiment with new skills. Keep introducing new ideas and, if the child is not ready, reintroduce those skills at another time.

Keep a close eye on the variations written after the activities, because many times they could be the key to integrating your program. Some activities have been around for ages and may seem overused, but the variation following the activity will show new and exciting ways to use some of your "old favorites."

Just about anything you do with your children can be turned into a positive learning experience. Be creative, teach, spend quality time together, relax, and most of all, have fun!

Dedication and Acknowledgments

This book is dedicated to my loving husband, Jeff,
for his patience, advice, friendship, support, and computer assistance.
Thanks for everything!

Thanks to my children, Kim and Tyler, for their understanding while I spent time away from them to create this book and for sharing me with other children. Thanks to all my family and friends who gave me support along the way.

Special acknowledgment is gratefully accorded to Wildwood Resources, Inc. for their permission to use their nutritional information and for unselfishly teaching me about nutrition over the years.

...and to all the children that have come into my life and helped me to grow and to create.

This book was inspired by all the children I have never met but had the need to reach in some way.

About The Author

Denise S. Theobald first recognized the value of learning while playing school with her big sister when they were just young children. She began baby-sitting at the age of eleven. Those experiences led her to a Bachelor of Science degree in Elementary Education from the University of Colorado and continuing graduate work in education at the University of Northern Colorado. Denise has several years of experience teaching kindergarten and summer programs with school age children. For more than thirteen years, she has owned and operated a professional licensed child care home and preschool. Working as a part-time professional artist has occupied much of her past eighteen years. She has belonged to state and county child care associations, and several city and county art leagues which have shown, judged, and sold much of her artwork. Currently, she is teaching in an all-day kindergarten. Most importantly, she has a life-long commitment towards giving to children.

Home is a very special place to Denise. During her years of teaching at home, she worked, lived, and breathed there with her "more than understanding" husband, and two children who benefited from the constant attention and teaching they received. Half of their home looked like a home and the other half looked like a classroom. The children in her care felt the combination and excitement in having a little of both worlds.

Denise felt the need to pass on valuable information and creative ideas to other parents and professional providers, so HOMESPUN CURRICULUM has been written to reach children that are beyond her daily care. She is dedicated to her profession and believes children everywhere should be given more chances at growing and learning.

Table Of Contents

Part II: Fun is Educational: Pre-Educational Activities, Foundations, and Reinforcement

Part III: Creative Genius

Chapter 7: Creating is Elating - Arts and Crafts

Chapter 8: Magical Outlets - Music/Dramatics

Chapter 9:   Learning With Food - Nutrition

Chapter l0:   Fun for Everyone - Creative Play and Games

Part IV: Potpourri: Yearly Activities to Integrate into the Curriculum

Chapter 11: Holiday Celebrations

References

Chapter 1:

Suggestions on Organizing Activities

Chapter 1 Introduction

Getting organized is always the first step in planning any curriculum. To help you get started, look over the daily schedule suggestions and detailed developmental sample outlines at the beginning of this chapter. Use these suggestions for your own daily schedule, or as guidelines for designing what fits your own needs. A monthly calendar sample is included to help give you an idea of how to plan activities once you have decided upon your goals for the children. A blank master calendar is available for copying and using for your month-to-month plans. For those of you who feel you have less than adequate artistic abilities, no need to worry! This chapter will give you confidence in your creative talents. HOW TO MODIFY AND INTEGRATE ACTIVITIES is the foundation of the book because this section describes how to change activities to fit the needs of all ages of children. Here you will find explanations of the picture codes that are used throughout this book. These picture codes will offer you quick references for infant, toddler, and school-age variations of activities. If necessary, check the broad reference list to help you get acquainted with the development of infants and toddlers.

GETTING ORGANIZED

The first step in organizing yourself is setting goals. Decide upon the amount of developmental activities you want to accomplish daily with your children. Make a list of daily chores you need to fit into the daily schedule. Write a rough draft of the day. Children need to have some structure in their lives and this helps you to become more organized, too. Remember, this is just a sample; be sure your daily schedule fits your needs!

TIME	PLANS/KIDS	PLANS/YOU
7:00 am	eat, dress, free-play	dishes, chores
8:30 am	creative play	supervise/prepare activities
9:00 am	activity #1	teach lesson/activity #1
9:45 am	snacktime/bathroom break	prepare snack and serve
10:00 am	activity #2	teach lesson/activity #2
10:45 am	outside time	supervise outside time
11:00 am	free-play, educational TV, read	prepare lunch
11:30 am	lunch time	lunch time
12:00 pm	quiet reading	clean-up
12:30 pm	storytime	storytime
1:00 pm	naptime	free-time; relax or do planning
2:30 pm	kids get up/bathroom time	prepare snack
3:00 pm	snacktime/outside activities	snacktime/outside supervision
3:30 pm to 5:00 pm	pick and choose-creative play, stories, centers, activities	allow choice and flexibility; plan field trip, centers, extra activities, etc.

DEVELOPMENTAL PLANS

Now that there is a daily structure, start planning what you want to accomplish over a longer period of time. An excellent way to structure the year is to divide it into three periods of four-months each; Fall, Spring, and Summer work nicely. On a piece of paper, write each child's name and, under each name, write the developmental areas you wish to work on with each child. You can assess each child's areas of need using an assessment tool like *Humanics Assessment Tests*; there are three different tests, one for ages 0-3, one for 3-6, and one for 6-9. These thorough assessments examine each of the five developmental areas with easy activities that fit into everyday life, and anyone can administer the test for the results to be accurate. Below is an informal sample of how to individualize developmental plans.

Tyler/Heather	Kimberly/Bobby
READING	**READING**
letter recognition rhyming creating stories story sequencing writing skills address/phone listening skills comparisons (opposites)	vocabulary building alphabet (beginning) story sequencing rhymes/songs stories discrimination (in-out, up-down, same/different) listening skills picture recognition
MATH	**MATH**
patterns/sequencing/sets number recognition counting by 10's writing numbers problem-solving beginning adding	patterns counting colors shapes simple puzzles
SOCIAL STUDIES/SCIENCE/ART	**SOCIAL STUDIES/SCIENCE/ART**
hand-eye coordination cutting, gluing, drawing, writing social skills creativity culture comparisons including family, self. animals (habitats and behavior)	hand-eye coordination cutting, gluing, coloring social skills building (blocks, paper) culture comparisons including family, self. animals (characteristics and recognition)
MUSIC/DRAMA/NUTRITION/GAMES	**MUSIC/DRAMA/NUTRITION/GAMES**
rhythm role playing large motor development food groups	rhythm movement large motor development food groups

Now that you have decided upon types of development objectives for each child, decide what days of the week you will teach certain subjects. Write those at the top of your monthly calendar. Find activities that will coincide with weekly subjects and developmental objectives. Review the sample monthly calendar below (showing daily subjects, objectives, and sample activities), then make copies of the blank monthly calendar and begin structuring your curriculum.

SEPTEMBER				
Reading & Science	Math & Arts/Crafts	Reading Music/Drama and/or Nutrition	Math & Social Studies	Creative Play & Misc.
MONDAY	TUESDAY	WEDNESDAY	THURSDAY	FRIDAY
Alphabet Annie Letter Pp Letter Kites *letter recognition Pets *animal behavior and habitats	Count the Shoes *number recognition and counting Painting pictures of pets *hand-eye coord.	Picture That! *picture recognition Restaurant *food groups	It's Me! *self-awareness Shape Mobiles *color and shape recognition	Set up a pretend pet store *role-playing Field Trip to local pet store
Alphabet Annie Letter Tt Letter Fruit Trees *letter recognition Library Trip Dinosaur Week research books	Counting and graphing gummy dinosaurs *counting, sorting and graphing Clay dinosaurs *creativity and fine motor skills	Sequencing Stories-Little Red Riding Hood *story sequencing & comprehension Rhythm instruments *rhythm	My Favorites *social skills/self Counting Books *number recognition	Centers blocks, record books, lacing cards, painting Game-Bing' *picture recognition
Alphabet Annie Letter Rr ABC Day *letter recognition Dinosaur story & dinosaur eggs *animals	Homemade Abacus & counting *counting l-10 Painting dinosaurs *creativity and theme reinforced	Simon Says *same/different 'Molden Oldies' *problem-solving and deduction and nutrition	Family Portraits *social awareness & self A "Leafy" Sort *sorting/shapes & sets	Library Visit *library skills/reading& language Storytelling Ping-Pong Races *large motor
Alphabet Annie Letter Aa Salt & Pepper letter recognition Ocean Animals *characteristics/ silhouettes	The Octopus *#'s l-8 Hats Match *careers, Labor Day and creativity	Nursery Rhyme Mosaics *rhyming Silly Songs *listening and comprehension	Job Scene *career awareness & social skills Five Little Turtles *counting & recognition	Shell Mosaics *design Ocean Voyage *role-playing & creativity

MONTHLY CALENDAR

MONDAY	TUESDAY	WEDNESDAY	THURSDAY	FRIDAY

19

ORGANIZING YOUR TIME

There are several ways to organize time for weekly preparation after your monthly outline is completed. You can choose from "monthly," "weekly," "the night before", or "last minute" preparations.

MONTHLY: After completing your calendar outlines, spend a weekend preparing the following month. Using an empty box or a file cabinet, file any necessary papers or prepared activities away so they will be at your fingertips daily. This method can be mind-boggling if you are not the over-ambitious type.

WEEKLY: Prepare activities over the weekend at your leisure and file. This method of preparation is perfect for the semi-ambitious person who may be a little short on time. This way gives you a lot of time to get ready, but does not rely on last minute preparations.

THE NIGHT BEFORE: Prepare your next day's activities while watching your favorite TV show or just while relaxing. This is great for the person who does not like last-minute details or who has a hard time getting organized in the morning.

LAST MINUTE: Prepare the day's activities after breakfast or before the kids get up in the morning, but be sure the kids are well-occupied because you will be interrupted. This is not the recommended method to use for being organized unless you are very quick with preparations and very patient with your children. If this is the only method that works for you and you don't feel rushed, then by all means, use this method.

BEING CREATIVE

The more you search for and utilize new ideas from available sources, the more comfortable and familiar you will become with teaching children at home. Creating your own ideas or changing ideas from outside resources will soon develop with experience. This is what creativity is all about.

If you pay close attention to your children, you will notice that they are developing many different skills all at the same time, but all from the same activity. After learning to develop your own mind into recognizing the potential of an activity, it is amazing to see just how much you teach children without even noticing. For example, when looking at the project called Jack O' Lantern Puzzles, the main idea is for the children to have fun making an arts and crafts project to celebrate Halloween. The main concepts listed in this activity are:

- ◆ spatial relationship (math)
- ◆ matching (math)
- ◆ hand-eye coordination

Upon further examination of this activity, additional concepts can be recognized. Here are just a few ideas:

- color/geometric shapes (ie: orange-black/triangle-circle
- creativity development
- facial relationships (eyes-nose-mouth-ears)
- counting (puzzle pieces)
- deductive reasoning ("That piece is too big to fit here.")
- problem-solving (fitting the pieces together)
- developing listening skills
- following directions
- fine motor development

When adding reading and language arts skills to this list, the lesson could be varied to include writing letters on the pumpkin pieces instead of drawing faces. Children could dictate stories about their jack o' lanterns. Science could become integrated by discussing the life of a pumpkin and follow up with a Nutrition lesson by baking pumpkin seeds or a pie. Teaching the children the history of the pumpkin as a jack o' lantern could be considered a Social Studies unit. When you use your imagination, the learning possibilities are numerous (and you thought the kids were making a simple pumpkin just for something to do!).

This book was not just intended as a resource book, but to provide you with a learning opportunity: you can be creative in formulating or adding to your curriculum. As you read through each activity in this book, you will begin to see the pattern of taking one idea and changing it slightly to fit totally different objectives. It just takes a little practice, but try it! Look at an activity in any resource book and see if you can alter it enough to fit it into a completely different subject or vary it to work with another age group.

Being creative makes some people nervous. Many think it means being able to paint like Rembrandt, so if they cannot draw, it means they are not creative. Don't worry about how talented you feel you are at drawing preparations for projects. Follow some of the guides or pictures in this book (and other books). The children probably see you as the greatest artist in the whole world. To help yourself feel more comfortable, choose easy pictures using basic shapes or little detail. Magazines are wonderful for the more difficult-to-draw pictures (ie: animals, food, people). With the homemade printer method shown in Chapter 2, make copies of your own worksheets at home. Trace nursery rhymes, pictures, animals, picture vocabulary ideas and other things without worrying about knowing how to draw. Just remember; be rewarded knowing that whatever you do with your children, they will benefit in some way. Start with projects that are comfortable and easy and, before you know it, you will be an expert!

CREATING AN INTEGRATED LESSON USING AN EXISTING STORY OR THEME

Look for a book or think of a theme (such as transportation, particular foods, entertainment, animals, the circus, friends, etc.). There are endless themes and books out there just waiting for you to use. When you have decided upon a book or theme, write down different subject areas, objectives and/or concepts you want to cover in your curriculum. Once these have been established, create activities or get resource materials to help plan the integrated lesson. Here is a step-by-step example of an integrated lesson.

LITERATURE BASED LESSON-STORY:

1. Choose a book or theme: Read the story, *The Little Mouse, the Red Ripe Strawberry, and the Big Hungry Bear* by Don and Audry Wood. (Check this book out of your local library or buy it in the children's section of your local bookstore)

2. Decide upon subject areas possible: Reading, Language, Arts, Science, Nutrition, Math, Art, and Drama.

3. Decide upon concepts or objectives depending upon age groups. **Reading**: listening skills, comprehension; **Language Arts**: vocabulary, speech, expression; **Science**: plants; **Nutrition**: fruit group; **Math**: counting, fractions; **Art**: fine motor skills, perception, color; **Drama**: recreating or role-playing from comprehension.

4. Make a list of activities (create or use resource books or materials) to fit the concepts or objectives.

- ◆ **Reading** - Read the story. Have the children dictate a sentence telling where they might hide a red, ripe strawberry ("If I had a strawberry, I would hide it_____.") and have them illustrate the page. With all the pages, make a big book.
- ◆ **Language Arts** - Ask questions, discuss concepts, review vocabulary words. Discuss whether the children think there really is a bear and who they think is telling the story.
- ◆ **Science** - Make a worksheet showing the parts of a strawberry plant. Draw the parts of the strawberry plant onto different colored construction paper and have the children cut out and glue onto paper. Plant strawberry seeds or visit a place that grows strawberries.
- ◆ **Nutrition** - Find a recipe that uses strawberries and make that dish together. Discuss the importance of fruits in the diet.
- ◆ **Math** - Count a dishful of strawberries (or add and subtract for older children). Write the number on paper. Draw that many strawberries on paper and write the number at the top of the page in black magic marker. Cut strawberries in half to teach two halves make a whole. Try cutting further to teach quarters.
- ◆ **Art** - Using a balloon and the recipe for papier-mache', create a strawberry. After drying a few days, paint the strawberry red. Glue black construction paper seeds all over the strawberry. Add green construction paper leaves.

◆ **Drama** - Find props: glasses or similar mask from book, strawberries, table knife, chain and lock, tablecloth, spoon, and paper construction strawberry. Have one child be the mouse and one be the bear (never to really enter the story). Read the story and let the children act out as you read. Allow the mouse to share the strawberry with you, the narrator. Switch actors and try the story again! If there are many children in your group, they will all want a chance. Possibly one of them will know the story well enough to narrate from memory, or an older child can be the narrator.

5. Now it's time to get materials together and decide on when and how many days it will take to complete these story activities.

The preparation and planning are completed. You have an integrated lesson. Just follow your lesson and the kids will be gaining and learning so much! Try this step-by-step procedure with other stories for practice. Then go on to themes. It is easy, especially after practicing, and <u>you can do it!</u>

HOW TO MODIFY & INTEGRATE ACTIVITIES

The activities in this curriculum are for children under the age of twelve. Most activities are written for the preschool and kindergarten group and can be modified for the younger and/or older groups. These groupings are not "carved in stone" according to ages. Use your best judgment when choosing activities for any child , even if they should fall under a specific grouping. Some may be ready for more, and some may require less. Know the capabilities of each child. Some kindergarten children will be ready for school-age activities and some preschoolers may be working on toddler activities. The groupings in this book are basic guidelines. When an activity can be modified to meet the needs of a different group, it will be coded as such. When an activity is written for any age group, it will specify **ALL**. Below are the symbols that will be used throughout the book to show when each activity can be changed and which age groups can participate.

INFANT   **TODDLER**   **SCHOOL-AGE**

To get accustomed to modifying activities among a varied age group, begin by using the activities provided for you in this curriculum guide. After you have become familiar with some of these activities and want to change activities from other resources, the best way is to be aware of the developmental capabilities of the groups. The groups that are the most difficult to modify are the infant and toddler, because they are limited in the skills that are required for many structured projects. To get more acquainted with the development of these groups, here is a list of some basic areas to consider when planning your activities.

INFANTS AND YOUNG TODDLERS

- imitation of sounds, words, actions (stories, nursery rhymes, imitation games, peek-a-boo, singing, animal sounds, talking)
- action repetition (building games, imitation games (like patty cake), water play)
- fine motor development (picking up small items, touching exploration, stacking, grasping, beginning crayon and pasting, ball)
- language development (nursery rhymes, stories, music, singing, imitation, listening games)
- visual discrimination (exploring objects, pictures, mobiles, easy puzzles)
- large motor development (imitation games, throwing, clapping, dancing)
- object recognition (explore inside and outside of home while naming and describing objects, searching games, pictures and books)
- self-image development (mirrors, touching, name games and songs, parts of the body)
- spatial relationship (putting objects into containers, stacking, hide and seek)
- memory development (hide objects, reading stories, repetition, water and sand play, singing games, animal sounds and pictures, easy puzzles, talking and descriptive activities)

OLDER TODDLERS

- imitation of words, sentences, actions (stories, rhymes, repetition poems, felt board stories, puppets, games, vocabulary building, following directions)
- visual discrimination (picture recognition, beginning colors and shapes, body and facial parts, puzzles, building, identification of objects and usefulness)
- fine motor skills (coloring, drawing, playdough, painting, gluing, lacing, beginning cutting)
- spatial relationships (in/out, up/down, around/up/under activities, containers, dancing, imitation games, building)
- memory development (vocabulary building, following simple directions, sentence building, easy counting, whisper games, hiding games, naming, same/different, animal sounds, nursery rhymes, shape recognition, sorting)
- problem-solving (beginning patterns, easy puzzles, building, grouping, group discussions, crafts)
- large motor skills (imitation games, jumping, throwing, galloping, dancing, running, drama)

This is just a very simplified overview of development and ideas. Of course, even though infants are infants for a very short time, most activities are for older infants and not newborns. Use your best judgment. From the very beginning of life, children are being stimulated by their surroundings (even in the womb). Talking to your children in complete sentences, no matter how young they are, is very important. Good communication and language skills develop better and more quickly by using normal speech instead of "baby talk". Experiment with the children as individuals to see what best fits their needs. Know the child's capabilities and be patient. Some things just need exposure and take longer periods of development (cutting with scissors cannot be mastered overnight!).

CHAPTER 2:

Helpful Hints, Recipes, and Materials

Chapter 2 Introduction

The purpose of this chapter is to bring together supplementary materials that reinforce the activities and concepts used throughout this book. When developing a program to use with children, it is easier and more convenient to have resources right at your fingertips!

Recipes for materials and techniques are included to help cut costs, make activities more accessible, and increase the creativity of the teacher and children. The homemade "printer" recipe is probably the most valuable recipe in this book. Although the initial expense of the "printer" will be the most costly of your materials, the printer is worth every penny. It can be used to make copies of the patterns and worksheets that follow, to create your very own worksheets, and to reproduce anything of interest and significance to your program.

The patterns throughout the book can be utilized to trace or to make copies using either a copy machine or the homemade printing method. The patterns and worksheets are drawn simply and can be used to create more related activities; be creative and go beyond the activities here!

To further assist you in your curriculum development, refer to the suggested references at the end of this book. Computer programs for all ages and areas of learning are included to reinforce or introduce concepts that you will be developing in your program. The book reference list includes various subjects which will help you build on to your program in the future.

Your ability to create an exciting and rewarding enrichment curriculum for your children is just as available to you as this book. Enjoy using these materials and ideas to help you design a program that fits your needs and the needs of the precious children who surround you every day.

This section of the book will give you some suggestions in using a few of the basic media that will be applied in many of the projects included in future chapters. The following methods show how to introduce and teach the skills and media to very young children with no experience.

GLUING

Gluing is used most often in this book because it is one of the easiest skills for very young children to learn. Gluing opens a whole world of activities for toddlers and preschoolers, yet is a skill that brings continued enjoyment for all ages.

There are four steps recommended for teaching children how to glue. Method 1 is for the youngest beginner; the methods progress through Method 4, for the experienced preschooler or school age child.

Method 1

Put the glue where _you_ want the object to go.

Give the child the object and tell them to place it onto the glue (point to the spot of glue)

Have the child pat the object to secure.

This is the way your toddlers will be gluing until the concept is understood.

Method 2

Hand the child the object.

Put the glue on the back for them, making sure to tell them you are turning the object over to put glue on the back. If this is repeated enough, the child will know to turn over a picture when beginning to glue on their own.

Point to where the object goes.

Have them pat the object to secure.

Now that the children have the routine of Methods 1 and 2, they are ready for some "independent" gluing. If you start Method 1 at an early age (12 months), by 18 months a child may be ready for this step. Use your own judgment on the child's readiness.

Method 3

Cut paper plates in half and pour some glue in the middle.

With a cotton swab, show them how to dip the end into the glue and onto the back of the object to be glued.

The children place the object where _they_ want it to go and pat.

Method 4 is for kindergartners and school age children. This definitely could be called the "normal" way for most people to glue, but believe it or not, some adults may even find this method a tad messy sometimes. Method 3 is still a better way for most preschoolers because glue is more uniform and the results are much neater.

Method 4

Children squeeze the glue straight from the bottle at a slant.

Remind children to use just a "dab" because too much glue will make their projects messy and will not stick as well.

PAINTING

Be sure to prepare the work area with newspapers and dress the children in smocks before attempting painting activities. One suggestion for smoother painting with young children is to purchase special spill-proof paint cups with covers that can be purchased through a school supply company. These are great to put water in for watercolor painting or paint in for tempera painting.

With masking tape, tape the painting papers to the work surface so the children can concentrate on painting and not worry about holding their papers still. Painting is a wonderful medium for learning other subjects and develops fine motor skills and creativity.

FINGER-PAINTING

Finger-painting is the easiest type of painting to introduce (and the messiest!). You can either buy finger paint or use the recipe given later in this chapter. Give your child one color at a time and rotate colors. Show them how to put their fingers into the paint and direct their hands to the paper. This is all the teaching necessary because they do catch on quickly.

WATERCOLORS

Use inexpensive boxes of watercolors with brushes included. Be sure to buy a box for every child and write their names on each. Have the child hold the brush like a crayon. Hold their hands and show them how to dip the brush into the water, swish the brush into the color, and direct their hands to the paper. Go through the sequence with them many times, always telling them the steps out loud. The toddlers will tend to be more interested in dipping only into the water and forget about the paint. That is fine.

They will need help remembering to put paint on their brushes for a while, so allow them to have fun while learning the procedures. Do not worry about having the children paint something in particular until they have mastered the skill.

MAGAZINE COLLAGES

Magazines are an invaluable resource for all kinds of activities. Collages can be made from magazine cut-outs in all subject areas. Here are some ideas for collages and the categories of developmental subjects:

COLLAGE	DEVELOPMENTAL SUBJECT
◆ animals	Science
◆ transportation	Social Studies
◆ machines	Science
◆ food	Science/Nutrition
◆ same-different	Math/Reading
◆ size comparison	Math
◆ letter recognition	Reading
◆ number recognition	Math
◆ picture vocabulary	Reading
◆ scavenger hunts	Games
◆ holiday pictures	Holidays
◆ people	Social Studies
◆ parts of the body	Science
◆ feelings	Social Studies
◆ designs	Arts and Crafts
◆ shapes/colors	Math
◆ counting/numbers	Math
◆ clothes	Social Studies
◆ toys	Creative Play

Recipes

The following recipes can be used to design your own activities or to assist you in activities throughout this book.

PAPIER-MÂCHÉ

Papier-mâché is an all time favorite activity. The recipe is given later in this chapter. Give each child his or her own little bowls of paste. Hand the children the wet strip and, while holding their hands, guide their strips to the object that is being covered. Show the children how to smooth down the paper. Preschoolers begin working independently very quickly. Toddlers will get the idea, too, but need assistance. Children as young as twelve months can even have fun being involved. After toddlers have placed five or six strips all by themselves, they may get bored and leave the rest to you, so be prepared. It seems like a big mess but it is so worth the effort. It is fun for them and will bring you fond memories, so get out the cameras (if you can find time to wash your hands!).

The Homemade Printer

This process can save much work and time. Using ditto masters, you can make up your own worksheets, newsletters, and art activities. For multiple copies of any kind, follow this recipe:

Ingredients:
        6 envelopes of unflavored gelatin
        1/2 Cup cold water
        4 1/2 Tbs. sugar
        1 1/2 Pints of glycerin (without rosewater)

Other materials needed: ditto masters, paper, pen and a cookie sheet specifically to use only for the printer.

Directions: Boil the first four ingredients and pour the mixture onto a cookie sheet. Wipe the bubbles off with a straight edged piece of cardboard. Cool and let set for 24 hours before using.

To Use: Prepare a ditto master (buy a box at a school supply or office supply store) for a worksheet or whatever needs to be copied. Moisten the surface gently with a damp sponge. Press the ditto master lightly onto the gel and rub gently for a few minutes. Remove the ditto master from the gel. To print your copies, carefully lower a piece of blank paper onto the gel in the same position as the ditto master. There is one copy! Make as many copies as you wish. Wipe the gel with a sponge when finished. Wait 24 hours to make your next copy so the ink settles into the gel. If the gel surface becomes bumpy or irregular, just stick the cookie sheet back into a warm oven to smooth. Cool, and it is ready for reuse.

Hints: If possible, purchase the largest cookie sheet you can find, so two ditto sheets can be reproduced at the same time, side by side.

Homemade Rainbow Crayons

Directions: Go through all those buckets and boxes of crayons to find all the broken pieces no one ever wants to use. Place these pieces into a leftover pie tin or pie plate. Bake at 200 degrees until all the crayons are melted. Cool and break into smaller crayons. Look at the fancy and unique results of multicolored crayons!

Homemade Paint/Glazing

This paint can be used on paper and on cookies (it is edible). Use for finger paints or brush painting. It has a shiny finish and a yummy taste!

Ingredients:
      food color
      corn syrup
      bowls

Directions: Pour desired amount of syrup into many different bowls. Put several drops of food coloring into each bowl (use a different color in each bowl) and stir. It is now ready for the painting of your choice.

Glazing: When a shiny effect is desired on any finished paper art activity, just brush on a little corn syrup, sparingly, until covered. Let dry.

Papier-Mâché Paste

This is enough paste to cover 2 to 3 medium sized balloons.

Ingredients:
      1 1/2 Cup flour
      2 Cups warm water

Mix flour and water into a large bowl (avoid plastic, lightweight bowls that tip easily). Tear strips of newspaper approximately 2" by 12". For younger children, use 2" by 6" strips. Dip into the paste. Lift the strip with one hand. Using the other hand, starting from the top, slide your fingers downward to wipe off the excess paste. Smooth the strip over the object that is being covered. Balloons are the most popular base for papier-mâché'. Other sculptures can be obtained by crumpling up newspaper onto a flat surface, covering with waxed paper and then molding the paper strips around the shape.

Silly Dough

This is extremely fun for children to make. Experiment with the measurements of the ingredients to get a satisfactory consistency.

Ingredients:
      liquid starch
      white glue
      food coloring

Natural Dyes

The following colors can be made and used in art projects, homemade greeting cards, and paper pictures. Other subject areas can be reinforced by studying each natural dye.

Ingredients:
blue - blueberries; red cabbage
pink - beets; strawberries
orange - carrot juice; orange peel
gold - onion skins
yellow - curry powder; lemon peel; dandelion flowers
green - spinach and other dark green leafy foods

Directions: Using a garlic press or mortal and pestle, grind the chosen ingredients. Use a paint brush, fingers, or cotton swabs as tools.

Laminating

Most homes or small businesses are not fortunate enough to have access to real laminating equipment. To buy the equipment and materials would be extremely costly. It just seems that we all need to use one for making learning cards, games and game boards, gifts and other manipulatives. Well, breathe easier. Although the following method may not be "as good" as the fancy machines, it surely gets the job done. At your local discount store, you can reasonably purchase clear shelf paper by the roll. This is great to use on all those projects that need preserving.

Directions: Simply cut the amount of paper necessary to cover the object, peel off the paper backing, and lay the object on the sticky side. Use a flat surface. Cut an equal amount of paper to cover the other side of the object in the same manner.

Peanut Butter Play Dough

This is an edible project the kids will definitely not want to miss!

Ingredients:
18 ounces of peanut butter
6 Tbs.. honey
mix dry powdered milk to desired consistency

Directions: Mix ingredients thoroughly. If the dough is too sticky, add more powdered milk. If it is too dry, add a little honey. Separate the dough into little balls for each child. Store in a baggy with each child's name or let them indulge before or after they are finished playing and creating.

Homemade Art Dough

This dough is more like the kind that can be purchased, but is considerably cheaper. It stores well for a week in a zipper lock bag in the refrigerator. When the children are finished playing with the dough, have them create something to cook and keep.

Ingredients:

4 c. flour
1 c. salt
1 1/2 c. warm water

Directions: Mix flour and salt together. Add water and stir until moistened. Place on floured board and knead until smooth (6 to 10 minutes).

Baking: Roll dough about 1/4 inch for artwork. Bake in two stages. Preliminary short baking is for setting the form. Trim is added and then baked to "rock" hardness. Bake the art work at 250 degrees and check periodically. If there are signs of over browning, wrap loosely in foil and finish baking. Prick bubbles during baking with a toothpick. If desired, spray with a clear polyethylene spray varnish for a finished look.

BUY AND KEEP ON HAND

- construction paper (all colors)
- glue
- rounded scissors for kids
- sharp scissors for adults
- white paper
- watercolors/brushes
- crayons/markers
- tape (masking/clear)
- tempera paint
- paper punch
- ruler
- hot glue gun/glue sticks
- glitter
- brushes
- cotton swabs

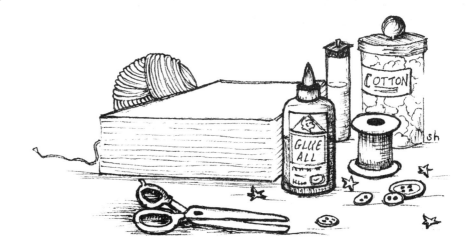

COLLECT AND SAVE

- buttons
- zippers
- newspapers
- oatmeal containers
- baby food jars
- film canisters
- wrapping paper
- tin pie plates
- cotton balls
- paper plates
- lunch sacks
- felt
- food coloring
- shelf paper (clear)
- paper towel tubes
- fabric scraps
- thread spools
- cardboard
- egg cartons
- milk cartons
- ribbons
- yarn
- plastic bottles
- old greeting cards
- clothespins
- Styrofoam
- foil
- wax paper
- packages of eyes
- coffee cans
- paper cups
- paper tubes

UTILIZING STORE BOUGHT WORKBOOKS

Buy inexpensive preschool workbooks, dot-to-dots, activity books, and coloring books. Utilizing a copy machine or the homemade method of printing copies shown in this chapter, make copies of activities to do with the children. Workbooks are useful for getting more ideas and patterns to copy for future activities. The workbook activities can also be used as follow-up exercises for reinforcing letters, numbers, sounds, picture recognition, color recognition, word development, and many other areas of learning.

GATHERING IDEAS

In the library, there are numerous books that have arts, crafts, science, and other subjects for children. Start a file box using index cards. Thumb through books to see activities of interest to you and your children. You will soon be able to categorize activities easily into subject areas. Write down those activities that will fit into the needs of your teaching plan.

ONE LAST HINT

Use a thick, black magic marker when preparing drawings for children to cut out. The black is bold, easier for them to see, they'll make fewer cutting mistakes, and it gives a nicer, finished look to their projects.

BEHAVIOR MODIFICATION

When you are ready to begin an activity with the children, let them know in an exciting manner that it is almost time to begin a project. It is usually an exciting time for them, so they should not have any trouble picking up their toys; nor should getting their attention be a problem. However, it is much easier to be successful at structured activities when certain behaviors are kept under control and when children cooperate. This section describes some techniques to help accomplish more positive behavior.

MATERIALS: one sheet of poster board
10" circle cut from cardboard
fasteners

PREPARATIONS: Decide what responsibilities you expect the children to accomplish after projects or playtime. With a marker, section the circle like a pie and write each child's name in an area. Punch a hole in the center of the wheel with a paper fastener so it moves easily but firmly. Next, draw easy samples of the chores onto the poster board coinciding with the names on the wheel. When the wheel is completed, explain to the children that, each day, they will switch responsibilities by turning the wheel. One child will always have a turn at the 'free day' and can sit back with nothing to do. If there is a responsibility that merits more than one person, then put two areas on the work wheel. This is a very good incentive for the children and keeps order when it is clean-up time. (Note: If one child has made an unnecessary, extreme mess, encourage them to assist the helper of the day.)

VARIATION: Have each child trace his or her hand from construction paper. They can cut the hand pattern out and glue onto the wheel. Write their names on the hand silhouettes.

Busy List

During those lull times in the day when the children have free play but cannot seem to find anything to do, gather them around and discuss all their ideas about keeping busy. Find out what they enjoy and write a list of things to do, adding a few ideas of your own. Then, on a large rectangular shaped paper, posterboard, or construction paper (taped together if necessary), draw circles for balloons (or squares for blocks, etc.). Categorize their ideas into each balloon by writing, drawing, or cutting out pictures.

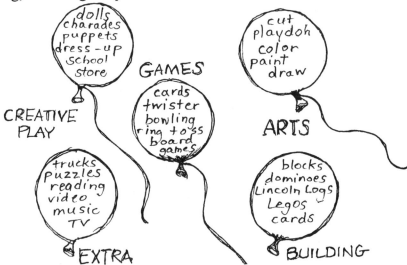

Whenever the children seem to be at a loss for something to do or they are acting a bit unruly, direct them towards the busy list and encourage them to choose something to do.

Signs

Certain behaviors seem to pop up constantly when several children are involved. Redirecting behavior is a wonderful way to curb unwanted behavior. Redirecting, however, means that you are the one who is always responsible for controlling the child's behavior, instead of putting some of the responsibility for the behavior onto them. This activity involves children helping themselves to become more under control on their own.

MATERIALS: markers
                 construction paper

PREPARATION: With a black marker, trace around a dinner plate onto construction paper.

ACTIVITY: Gather the children around and have an open discussion on behaviors that need attention. Ask each child what behavior they need to work on most. Give the children two sheets of paper with circles. Let them decide one behavior they would like to keep under control and assign them one that you would like to see improve. Give them pencils to draw those behaviors inside the circles. With markers or crayons, they can color their pictures. Then draw a straight line across the picture and have them trace the line with black marker. Remind the children that these signs are just like the ones seen outside of the home (ie: no smoking, no pets).

The children can then hang their pictures at eye level around the areas of the house they feel the signs would be of most use to them.

SAMPLE SIGNS

WALKING ZONE

Bite-free zone (no biting sign)
Quiet zone (no loud voices sign)
Walking zone (no running sign)
Peaceful zone (no hitting sign)

It is amazing how much attention children pay to their own signs. You will not have to remind them about rules as often. This helps them recognize poor habits and encourages them to want to correct those habits on their own. They end up redirecting their own behavior!

MATERIALS: construction paper
scissors/markers
stickers (store bought)

PREPARATION: Outline an object the children enjoy, such as race cars, wagons, teddy bears, etc.

ACTIVITY: Have children cut out their shapes. Write each name in large letters on the shapes. Explain the particular behavior expected and, each time they are successful, let them put a sticker on the chart. Rewards can be given at the end of a certain time period (one day for younger children, several days for older children). There does not need to be a reward if you feel the chart is reward enough.

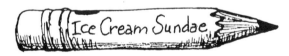

MATERIALS: paper
scissors
markers

PREPARATION: Draw a picture of an ice cream sundae on construction paper and cut it out. Buy or make stickers to use as sprinkles for toppings on the chart (ie: stars, cherries, candy).

ACTIVITY: Each time the child accomplishes the goal on the chart, add a topping to the sundae. When a certain amount of toppings have been added, take the child out for ice cream!

Behavior Signs

From construction paper, make as many empty ribbons, certificates, or any shaped awards as necessary. Discuss with the children types of behaviors on each award. Let them know that at the end of the day you will be handing out rewards to children who earn them. Decide which award each child earned for that day (they may earn more than one). If some children have a more difficult time with this than other children, make some of the awards easier to accomplish.

Children love to show these off to the other children. The more proud of their behavior they feel, the more they will want to continue striving towards mastering that particular behavior. Some children will earn all of the awards by the end of the week due to competitiveness. This is okay, too, as long as the competition does not get out of hand and others are not hurt in the process. This behavior modification has very satisfying results and can be used frequently when needed. Here are some award suggestions:

- ◆ **Outstanding!**
- ◆ **Good Housekeeping**
- ◆ **Friendly Playing**
- ◆ **Great Manners**
- ◆ **Very Cooperative!**
- ◆ **Follows the Rules**
- ◆ **Uses an Inside Voice**

Countdown to Cooperation

Kids love to race or compete; utilize this to get them to do what you want. Count to five (getting to the table), count to ten (to obtain silence), count to fifteen (to finish last minute picking up of toys) and continue raising the number for more time-consuming tasks. Try other techniques besides counting, ie: singing a song, saying the alphabet, etc. This works great and helps children learn as they cooperate!

Here are a few more suggestions on behavior modification.

1. Use positive reinforcement by observing the child and complimenting good behavior.
2. Give children physical activities to let out excess energy.
3. Redirect negative behavior by stopping problems before they occur. Move children away from problem situations and know what situations will cause future incidents so problems can be avoided.
4. Express an interest in what the children are doing. Be open and honest about situations.
5. If you see inappropriate behavior from one child, praise someone else who is exhibiting positive behavior (ie: 'I like the way Suzie is sharing'. If Bobby isn't sharing and he hears Suzie being praised for sharing, then it is likely he will correct his behavior to receive praise, too!).
6. Talk to your children.
7. Build positive self-images.
8. Set a good example for your children to follow.

Chapter 3:

ABC is Elementary-Reading

MATERIALS: paper (all colors)
tape/glue
scissors

PREPARATION: Enlarge the *Alphabet Annie* pattern below by drawing body parts on colored paper. Cut out all the parts. Choose a letter for the children to learn. Draw a capital and lower case of that letter to cut out.

ACTIVITY: Gather the children around the space on the wall where Annie will be placed. Lay all the pieces of Annie on the floor and have the children take turns finding each part. Start with the top of Annie and tape each part onto the wall until she is completed.

Choose someone to tape the capital letter to Annie's raised hand. Name the letter. The lower case letter can be taped to the lower hand. Name that letter. Remind the children daily what letters Annie is holding. Each week make new letters and have the children replace the old ones.

CONCEPTS:
◆ letter recognition
◆ body recognition
◆ capital and lower case differentiation

VARIATION:
Change *Alphabet Annie* to *Shape and Color Sharon*. Cut a different colored shape each week to learn colors and shapes. Annie can also become *Numbers Nelly, Adding Adelle, Multiplying Mona, Fractions Fran* and so on. Just use your imagination and she (or he, if you want to make a boy) can help to teach whatever age group or skill you want.

MATERIALS: sand/salt/pepper
cardboard or heavy paper

glue

PREPARATION: Write letters in marker on pieces of cardboard or paper.

ACTIVITY: With a glue bottle, children can trace the written letters in glue and sprinkle sand, or salt and pepper, over the glue. Tell the children the letter name. After the letters have dried, children can close their eyes, feel the shape, and guess the letter.

CONCEPTS:
- ◆ kinesthetic development
- ◆ fine motor skills
- ◆ letter recognition

VARIATION: Use shapes, words, or draw pictures and play a guessing game with ALL.

Letter Kites

MATERIALS: paper (2 colors)
glue
scissors/marker

PREPARATION: Draw a diamond shape for kites on 8 1/2" x 11" paper. Using a different color, cut 2" x 3" rectangles. Also cut letters out of different colors. Cut long, skinny strips from the other colored paper; cut as many as necessary for the letters to fit. Staple the strips together to make longer tails.

ACTIVITY: Have the children cut out their kites. For every five rectangles, they need one strip. Help them find the letters by saying "Can you find the letter 'B'?" (Often, it is easier to recognize letters after the name is said than it is to try to name the letter from memory.) Glue the letters onto the strips. When all the letters have been recognized or introduced and glued, staple the tail to the kite. Hang the kites where the children can easily review them for a few weeks.

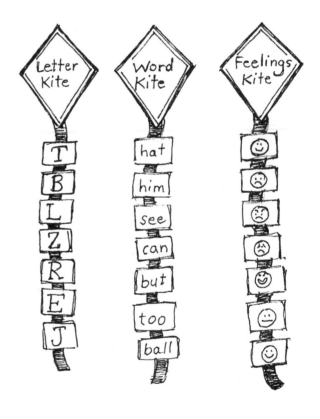

 Hang a feelings kite above the crib or wall where the infant can be visually stimulated. Show the feelings to the baby by saying the words "happy" or "sad"

43

while smiling or frowning.

 Make happy and sad faces on the squares to make feeling kites. Play a little copying game by pointing to faces and seeing how fast the children can change their expressions. Discuss what makes them happy and sad.

 School age children can make word kites. Easy words can be written for beginners and new vocabulary or spelling words can be used for more advanced readers.

VARIATION:
Use drawn or cut out pictures instead of feeling faces for infants and toddlers. Numbers, colors, or shapes can be used for the kite tail if a math activity is desired.

CONCEPTS:
- ◆ sequencing
- ◆ letter/word recognition
- ◆ facial discrimination
- ◆ fine motor development

MATERIALS: magazines
scissors
paper
glue

ACTIVITY: Ask children to look through magazines and cut out pictures of things they do not recognize. Have them glue their pictures to the paper. Write the name next to each picture and say the word aloud.

 While pointing to the pictures that you have pre-cut and glued, say the words.

Toddlers can glue the pictures that have been precut for them and can practice saying the words together with you.

 School age children can cut out pictures, write a story, and glue the pictures in sequence to match their story.

CONCEPTS:
- ◆ vocabulary building
- ◆ word recognition
- ◆ language development
- ◆ memory
- ◆ visual discrimination
- ◆ sequencing

MATERIALS: paper
index cards
markers

PREPARATION: Prepare cards with beginning letter sounds of different animals and silhouettes of those animals. Make a different set of cards with corresponding pictures (hand draw or cut out pictures).

ACTIVITY: Lay all the cards out face up and have children match the letters or silhouettes with the animals.

 For toddlers, just use the one set of animals and, after naming the animal, see if they can find the correct picture, and vice versa.

 Write the animals' names on one set of cards without the silhouettes. School age children can match the words and pictures. Then use just the picture cards and have them write down the names on paper to see if they can spell the words correctly. For extra fun, the children can draw other animals not included in your set of cards and try spelling their names. Have a dictionary handy so children can help themselves solve any difficulties in spelling.

CONCEPTS:
- picture, sounds, and letter recognition
- vocabulary/ spelling
- writing skills

VARIATION: Enhance memory skills by turning all the cards over and playing a game of memory. Children turn two cards over and try to find the animal and animal name that match. If they are correct, they keep those cards; if incorrect, the next person gets a turn. The one with the most cards wins.

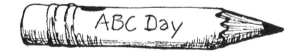

MATERIALS: 26 6" x 8" cards (heavy paper or cardboard)
pencils, crayons, markers
scissors
magazines
glue
construction paper (white and colored)

PREPARATION: Divide each card in half with a straight line made with magic marker. On each card, in the top area, write the upper and lower case letters (Aa-Zz; one card per letter).

Make booklets with colored covers. On each page, make a division line half way down. With a marker, write the upper and lower case letter in the upper left hand corner of each section.

ACTIVITY: Pick one day per week to have alphabet day. Have children look through magazines to find the letter that you are working on that day. Cut them out and glue on the page in the booklets under the area marked with that letter. Be sure to reinforce the name of the letters as they are working.

 School age children can illustrate the cardboard letter cards that you have prepared. Have them think of a word that begins with the letter on the card. As each illustrated card is completed, hang it on the wall. From time to time, ask the children to find a particular letter (or ask them to name the letters you point to). Do one or two letters per week.

CONCEPTS:
- ◆ letter recognition
- ◆ letter sounds
- ◆ creative thought
- ◆ fine motor development

VARIATION: Children can practice writing letters on lined tablet paper and glue them into their booklets.

MATERIALS: paper
pencils
crayons

ACTIVITY: Discuss special people (ie: grandparents, friends) with the children. Tell them you are going to write letters to a special person. Ask the children questions such as "What have you been doing that Grandma would like to know?" Give suggestions and write down everything. Using a children's writing tablet, print the letters neatly and read the letters back to the child. Have the children fold their letters and put on their own stamps. Make a special trip to the post office and later discuss how the letters will get to that person. Children can make pictures to go along with their letters.

 Toddlers can draw pictures and you can write short notes about them. They can do the folding and stamping.

 Older children who are capable of writing can try copying your printed letters themselves for practice. Those children just learning cursive can do their own.

CONCEPTS:
- verbal skills
- communication skills
- creative thought development
- writing skills
- listening skills
- exposure to social systems (postal service)

MATERIALS: sandpaper
velvet or any soft material
variety of scrap materials with different textures
glue
cardboard

ACTIVITY: Children glue different articles on their pieces of cardboard. After drying, the children close their eyes and feel the collages. While exploring the textures, they can be encouraged to describe what each thing feels like.

After making your infants a collage, hold them on your lap and let them feel the different textures. Describe these textures and talk about each item.

Allow toddlers to make their own collages with assistance. Describe the textures.

Older children can make a "feely" box to be used by all the children. Have them cut a hole in the side of a cardboard box, paint or decorate the box, and gather items to be secretly put inside. All the children will have fun describing and guessing what is in the box.

CONCEPTS:
- kinesthetic development
- descriptive vocabulary
- language development
- creative thought

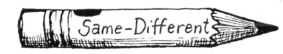

MATERIALS: paper
markers
pictures from coloring books or magazines

PREPARATION: Cut alike pictures of anything from magazines or coloring books or draw your own shapes and pictures on paper. For every two or three pictures, cut or draw a picture that is not alike (for example: triangle-triangle-square-triangle, or shoe-shoe-sandal-shoe). Glue or draw these pictures in horizontal sections across the page. Reproduce the worksheet for all of the children.

ACTIVITY: Gather the children at a table and discuss what same and different mean. Do the first worksheet together. The children can circle the pictures that are different and point to the ones that are the same. After children can see the differences between shapes and pictures, draw letters on the worksheets to begin the visual discrimination process of the alphabet.

CONCEPTS:
- ◆ problem-solving
- ◆ awareness of same/different/opposites
- ◆ following directions
- ◆ opposites

VARIATIONS: Make other worksheets, introducing such concepts as up-down, in-out, tall-short, above-under, etc. Be sure to discuss these; show examples and play games involving the concepts.

MATERIALS: construction paper
                        scissors
                        clear contact paper
                        pre-bought stickers

ACTIVITY: Children cut 2"x 6" strips of construction paper. Let them choose several stickers to decorate their bookmarks. When the bookmarks are decorated, help children cover them with contact paper. Show them how they can use the bookmarks during quiet reading.

 Make several colorful, laminated bookmarks for infants to grab and investigate.

 You will need to cut and laminate toddler bookmarks, but they will enjoy using stickers to decorate.

CONCEPTS:
- ◆ fine motor skills
- ◆ hand-eye coordination

VARIATIONS: Use pictures from magazines or self design bookmarkers with paint, crayons, or colored pencils.

MATERIALS: blue and white construction paper
scissors
markers

PREPARATION: Using a plate, draw large circles on white paper. Cut circles in half. With a marker, draw semi-circles to make arches of colors.

ACTIVITY: Children can color each section of their rainbow a different color, then glue the rainbows onto the blue background paper. You can write the poem on their papers or on index cards. Discuss rainbows and recite the poem together.

Make several smaller rainbows and attach them with string to a coat hanger. Hang where infant can see and recite the poem.

School age children can practice their writing skills by copying poems onto lined tablet paper.

CONCEPTS:
- language development
- memory
- verbal skills
- rhyme
- fine motor development

"RAINBOWS"
After the rain, there is Yellow, Orange, Green; It is the prettiest sight that you have ever seen! When the sun comes out it is magic in the sky: Blue, Indigo, Violet are the colors way up high.

VARIATIONS: This activity can be used as a Science or Art project with further study of weather or color combinations.

MATERIALS: colored construction paper
scissors
markers

PREPARATION: Draw footprints on paper (trace around an old shoe). Write letters on each footprint.

ACTIVITIES:
Children cut out the footprints and tape them all over the floor. Line up the children behind the

first print and call out a letter. The first child walks to that letter using the footprints. Call out another letter and have the next child walk to that letter, and so on until all the children finish the path to the end.

 Draw pictures or cut out pictures and glue onto footprints. Punch a hole at the top of each and string with yarn. Hang the footprints where your infant can see and tell him or her the name of each picture while pointing to it.

 Draw pictures or glue cutouts onto the footprints and have toddlers step from print to print as you call out the picture's name.

 Use words, phrases, or names of movies or books on the prints. Space the prints further apart on the floor for a more physically challenging game.

CONCEPTS:
- picture/letter/word recognition
- large motor development

VARIATION: For Math activity, use colors, shapes, numbers, or math facts. Science activities can have planets, plants and animals, or types of weather drawn on the prints. Social Studies activities for school age children can include famous dates in history, famous silhouettes, or pictures pertaining to different cultures.

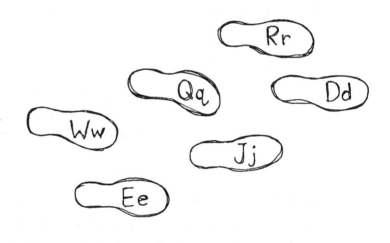

MATERIALS: pencil/paper
dictionary

PREPARATION: Write a list of words that are sure to be unknown to the children.

ACTIVITY: Read a new word to the children. Give the dictionary to one child and paper and pencil to all. The person who has the dictionary writes down the definition, while the other children write down a made-up meaning. The dictionary person reads all of the meanings aloud (including the real meaning). The children then vote on which definition is correct; once all votes are in, the real definition is read. Be sure everyone has a turn being the dictionary person.

CONCEPTS:
- spelling
- speech
- vocabulary

ACTIVITY: Once a week, gather the children into a group. Read five library books to the group. Have a group discussion about the books. Include questions like:

1. What was your favorite book?
2. What made this book good?
3. Why did you dislike this book?
4. What would you change to make the book better?

Have the children write and illustrate their own books using some of the solutions they discussed.

CONCEPTS:
- ◆ listening skills
- ◆ speech development
- ◆ group interaction
- ◆ problem-solving
- ◆ comprehension

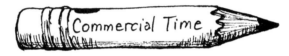

MATERIALS: pencil/paper
                    camera or video recorder

ACTIVITY: Have children pick a favorite product such as toys, food, drink, clothes. Discuss what they like about that product and have them think of ways to sell their product. Once the children have written down their ideas, they can write dialogue and decide upon props, costumes, and setting.

ALL: Act out the commercial, involving all children.

      Older children can use the camera or run the tape.

CONCEPTS:
- ◆ independent work
- ◆ language development
- ◆ writing skills
- ◆ creative expression

MATERIALS: paper
                    marker
                    prizes (stickers, edible treat, trinkets, IOU's for an outing)

PREPARATION: Prepare a map to a hidden treasure by drawing clues on paper. Each new place should have a new clue. Hide your prizes where the last clue stops.

 Involve infants by carrying them with you.

 Toddlers can help read the picture clues or make clues for them that are just pictures. Lead them step by step to each new clue.

 School age children should have more difficult clues using full sentences or detailed maps. When the treasure hunt is finished, encourage them to create their own instructions or maps to give to their friends to try.

CONCEPTS:
- ◆ visual perception
- ◆ following directions
- ◆ left-to-right sequencing
- ◆ creative thought
- ◆ problem-solving

MATERIALS: markers/pencil
paper
mirror

ACTIVITY: Children can write messages backwards on paper and let other children read them in mirrors.

CONCEPTS:
- ◆ creativity
- ◆ interpretation skills
- ◆ visual discrimination

VARIATION: With different coding methods, children can create secret messages using symbols or numbers for each letter in the alphabet. For more advanced coding, start the alphabet using a different letter. (If using the sample below, that means GAP would be spelled KET in secret code). Let the children write messages using their secret coding system.

-A-B-C-D-E-F-G-H-I-J-K-L-M-N-O-P-Q etc.

-E-F-G-H-I-J-K-L-M-N-O-P-Q-R-S-T-U- etc.

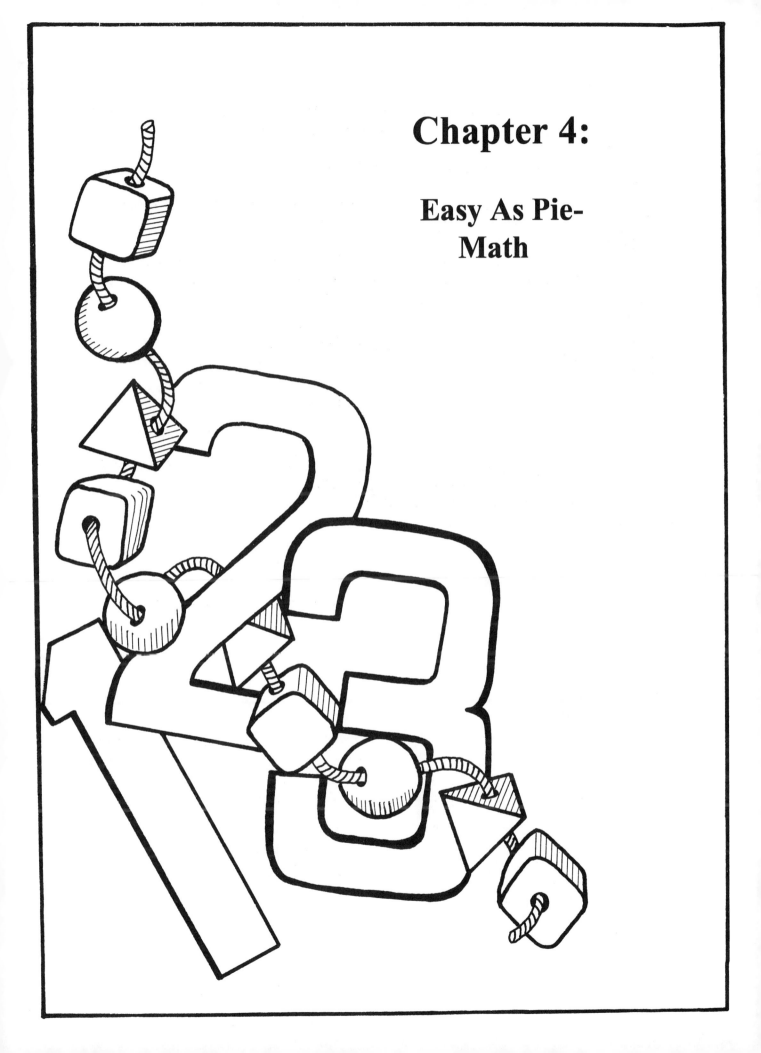

Chapter 4:

Easy As Pie-
Math

Chapter 4 Introduction

Simple Math activities can be exciting and fun for children of all ages. Over the years, parents have continually been trying to keep up with the ever-changing ways in which math is being taught. With school age children, we often need them show us what they are doing, while trying not to be too intimidated by having to learn new ways. But be reassured- this chapter's activities involve very basic concepts whose teaching has not changed. The pre-math curriculum touches on shapes, size comparison, sets/patterns, color, counting, number recognition, and a variety of simplified concepts that fit into the category of math. When using a variation for school age children, be sure to know how these concepts are being taught at your children's school so you can give them the best possible support.

MATERIALS: paper
glue
scissors
marker

PREPARATION: Draw pictures of things with different numbers of legs. Count the total number of legs and on a separate piece of paper, draw enough shoes for all the feet.

ACTIVITY: Children cut out all the shoes and glue them to the various feet (or pre-cut shoes for those children who cannot handle all that cutting!) Have children count the shoes. Watch them giggle when they see how funny those shoes look!

 Toddlers can match pre-cut shoes and glue.

Younger school age children and older preschoolers can add a combination of feet together to do concrete addition problems.

CONCEPTS:
- ◆ counting/adding
- ◆ number recognition
- ◆ fine motor skills
- ◆ matching

MATERIALS: store bought or handmade stickers
paper
marker

PREPARATION: Draw a picture of an octopus and write numbers 1-8 on each tentacle.

ACTIVITY: Tell the children that their octopus has many arms called tentacles. These tentacles are empty; let's put a sticker onto each tentacle. Each time they put a sticker on their octopus, have them count; do this until they have reached the number eight.

 Choose stickers that are simple and have contrast. As you put the stickers on the octopus for the infant, name each picture.

 Toddlers can participate in this activity without the numbers written on the tentacles.

 Draw several octopi on paper and write addition problems under each octopus. Children place the number of stickers according to the problem and add. Write the correct answer after the equal sign.

VARIATION: This could easily become a Science activity by following up with a study of octopi or other sea creatures. Find books about octopi for a Reading activity. Older children could write a story or a report.

CONCEPTS:
- ◆ counting
- ◆ adding
- ◆ number recognition
- ◆ vocabulary

MATERIALS: straws
cereal shaped like O's
yarn or string
scissors

PREPARATION: Precut straws into 1" pieces. Cut the yarn/string long enough to be tied into a necklace and slipped over a child's head. Tie one cereal to the bottom end of each string so the items will not fall off the string while the child is working.

ACTIVITY: Older preschoolers can sort and string while alternating cereal and straws into a simple pattern. Some children may be ready for more difficult patterning (ie; 2 straws, 1 cereal, 2 straws, 1 cereal, etc.). When the necklaces are completed, tie a knot and they are ready for wearing (or eating!).

 If your infants are older and eating some table food, put them in their high chairs with the cereal and let them practice their fine motor skills by playing and eating. With your supervision, give them an uncut straw and let them chew or blow through it.

Lacing is difficult at this stage, but you can put the string through the objects and have the child pull it through. Don't worry about patterns. They will be able to sort into piles with some help. With practice, they will be lacing by themselves.

Give school age children multiple items to lace and they will have fun making intricate patterns.

CONCEPTS:
- ◆ sorting
- ◆ patterns
- ◆ fine motor development
- ◆ hand-eye coordination
- ◆ problem-solving

MATERIALS: paper
marker
scissors
glue

PREPARATION: Trace five turtles onto each paper. Write a number on each turtle. Draw spots below the turtles.

ACTIVITY: Children cut out the turtle's spots and glue them to the turtle wearing that number.

Draw one big turtle for toddlers and pre-cut spots for them to glue and count with you.

CONCEPTS:
- ◆ counting
- ◆ number recognition
- ◆ language development

VARIATION: Include a Science activity by studying about turtles. Borrow someone's pet turtle or buy one from the pet store to make the project even more fun!

56

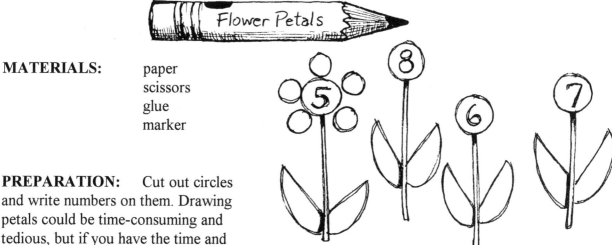

Flower Petals

MATERIALS: paper
scissors
glue
marker

PREPARATION: Cut out circles and write numbers on them. Drawing petals could be time-consuming and tedious, but if you have the time and patience, do so with the help of your school age children and preschoolers who know how to use scissors. If you do not want to draw and cut all of them, buy colored circle stickers for the children to use as petals. Draw stems and leaves for flowers.

ACTIVITY: Have the children glue a numbered circle on each stem. They can then count the petals and glue the correct number of petals around each numbered circle.

 Using brightly colored paper, make one large flower with a happy face in the circle. Attach the flower to the infant's crib for viewing.

 Toddlers can glue or stick petals on a few pre-drawn flowers. Count the petals aloud with the child.

 Have school age children find a storybook about flowers to read to the younger children.

CONCEPTS:
- ◆ counting
- ◆ number recognition
- ◆ fine motor development

cut petals

VARIATIONS: Study parts of the flower for a Science activity and plant seeds to grow flowers (egg cartons are great for this). Use stories or poems for Reading. Find out about your state flower and visit a botanical garden for follow up in a Social Studies activity. Using tissue paper and pipe cleaners, make flowers for an Art project.

Counting Books

MATERIALS: magazines
paper

scissors
glue
fasteners

PREPARATION: Make ten page booklets. Write numbers (1-10) at the top of each page.

ACTIVITY: Starting with number one, work on one number during each activity session. Have the children look through magazines and find that number in pictures. For example: one baby, one dog, one box of cereal; two pancakes, two people, two shoes; three cars, three houses, three trees; and on up through number ten. This project can be done once weekly until the book is completed.

 Each time you do this project with the other children, work on a booklet for your infant. Show the pictures and tell her the names of each picture. Count the pictures aloud to her; even though she will not understand counting, the verbal communication and exposure to the counting could be beneficial later.

 Instead of toddlers finding the correct number of pictures for each page, just have them cut random pictures and glue them to each page. Count with the child the number of pictures they have glued.

 Instead of a number at the top of each page, write an addition or subtraction problem. See if they can find pictures to correspond with that problem. After gluing the pictures next to the problem, the children can write the answer (ie: 2 + 3 = 2 babies + 3 babies = 5 babies).

CONCEPTS:
- number/ picture recognition
- counting
- addition/subtraction
- fine motor development

Manipulatives are "hands on" tools children use to develop thinking skills and help solve problems. Manipulatives can be used in all subjects, but are extremely effective when learning math skills. Here are some tools you can buy, make, or collect to teach counting, colors, patterns, sets, sorting, size, shapes, stacking, measuring, and number placement. Create projects with these tools or allow children to experiment and develop critical thinking skills. The list is endless. Look through school supply catalogs or educational stores for ideas. It is not necessary to spend a lot of money, because manipulatives can be made from household items once you have acquired the ideas. Allow children time during the day to use these materials. Decide what you want to teach and how you can use these materials to teach, then write up problems for the children to solve and allow the children to experiment with the materials daily.

shape boards	sorting	math games
abacus	materials	-dice
puzzles	-plastic animals	-Yahtzee
pegboard	-plastic shapes	-Chinese
beads/laces	-buttons	checkers
Unifix cubes	-spools	-Monopoly
measuring	-sugar cubes	-matching cards
devices	-macaroni	-Bingo
-cups	products	-Sorry!
-spoons	-dominoes	-building
-scales	-geoboards	materials
-containers	Cuisenaire rods	-blocks of all
-rulers	math cards	types and sizes

Counting Cards

MATERIALS: stickers or hand-drawn pictures
3" x 5" cards
markers

PREPARATION: Write one number (1-20) on each card.

ACTIVITY: Children glue pictures or attach stickers to the number on the card until all cards have the correct number of pictures to coincide with the numbers on the cards. Play a number game by spreading the cards out face up on the table. Children take turns choosing a card. If they can name the number on the card (allow them to count the pictures if necessary), they can keep that card.

 Make picture cards for infants. Talk to your child about each picture. They can hold their cards and examine them. If desired, laminate the cards with clear contact paper so chewing will not destroy them.

 Toddlers can play the same game, only using picture cards without numbers.

 The same game can be used with the cards for children learning addition or multiplication. Have the children choose two cards instead of one and add or multiply the two together. After a correct answer, they can keep both cards.

CONCEPTS:
- ◆ picture/ number recognition
- ◆ counting
- ◆ addition/ multiplication concepts
- ◆ vocabulary
- ◆ problem-solving

MATERIALS: colored paper
scissors

PREPARATION: Cut large shapes (triangles, circles, squares, rectangles, ovals, stars) from colored paper.

ACTIVITY: Giving specific directions, have the children put the different shapes into patterns. For example: square-circle-square-circle-square or oval, oval, triangle, oval, oval, triangle, and so on. Ask the children to find the shape that comes next. Continue the activity by changing the patterns or allowing them to create their own patterns.

CONCEPTS:
◆ shapes
◆ patterns
◆ problem-solving

VARIATIONS: Use dried foods instead of cut shapes to sort and make patterns. Use letters, numbers, or pictures, too. Collect other manipulatives for sorting (spools, buttons, paper clips, etc.) and store them in old margarine tubs for future use.

MATERIALS: 2-4 dice
paper
pencil

ACTIVITY: Children who are learning to count can roll the dice and count the dots. When they count correctly, draw a star on the paper under their names. Keep playing until the children are ready to quit. Add up their scores to see how well they have done. For children ready to learn adding and subtracting, roll the dice and add the numbers, or subtract smaller numbers from larger ones.

 Older children can use more than two dice and do multiple addition or use two dice to practice multiplication. Multiplication totals can be scored on paper and, after a limited number of rounds, have them add their own scores to practice double digit adding.

CONCEPTS:
◆ counting
◆ adding/subtracting
◆ multiplication

MATERIALS: colored construction paper
scissors
glue
marker

ACTIVITY: This project can be an ongoing activity or you can use any of the ideas as individual projects. Start with the number one and do a new number each week. When you have completed the desired amount, make number books. Change pictures for each number. The <u>WAGONS #1</u> activity below shows how to prepare and teach each number. Following this example are sample ideas of pictures, shapes, and numbers 2-10 that you can mix and match by using the same materials and directions.

WAGONS #1

Preparation: With a marker, divide construction paper into rectangles for a wagon body. Cut skinny rectangles for handles. Draw circles for wheels.

Activity: Ask children to find the wagon shape and glue it onto paper. Do the same with the wheels and handles. Write the number of wagons on the top of their papers. Count the wagons with the children. Review by asking the children the colors, shapes, number, and name of the object.

 Direct the child's gluing and ask him or her to name each picture. Count the pictures together. Stay under five items for older toddlers.

CONCEPTS:
◆ color/shape/number recognition
◆ counting
◆ vocabulary development
◆ fine motor development

#2

#1

#3

#4

61

#5

#6

#7

#8

#9

#10

MATERIALS: colored construction paper
markers
scissors
glue

PREPARATION: Draw a tree using green and brown paper (or trace a circle from green paper and a thin rectangle from brown). Draw apples on the red paper (or use any fruit; oranges are easy). Write a number on each piece of fruit.

ACTIVITY: Children cut out their numbered fruit and glue them onto the tree. Have them count the fruit and point to the numbers as they count.

 After preparing a tree for your infant, talk about the picture. Some older infants could sit on your lap and help you pat the fruit onto the tree.

 Omit the numbers on the fruit and let toddlers glue pre-cut fruit to the trees. Count the fruit together.

 Have older children design and prepare their own trees. They can use two trees to make up multiplication problems or division problems. Use the trees to do measuring activities (ie: How wide is your tree, how tall, compare trunk width and height with the fruit's width and height, graph measurements).

CONCEPTS:
- ◆ counting
- ◆ number recognition
- ◆ measuring
- ◆ multiplication/division
- ◆ fine motor development

VARIATIONS: As a follow-up Science activity, get a book from the library that shows pictures of different types of fruit and how they grow. Take a trip to an orchard. Have a Nutrition project by discussing the importance of fruit in our diet and following up with cooking applesauce or baking a fruit dish. Reading and Social Studies activities could involve a story about Johnny Appleseed or a trip to a canning factory. Have older children research how many different types of apples there are and make a follow up graph or poster presentation to share with the other children. During their research, have them find famous stories about apples (ie: Newton and gravity, William Tell, Snow White and the poisoned apple, etc.) and write a report with illustrations. Have the children illustrate how many different ways apples can be used and have them dictate. For a reading activity, write letters on the fruit, then write the matching letters on the green section of the tree. Have the children match the letters on the fruit to the letters on the tree and glue. Say the letter names together with the children.

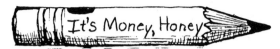

It's Money, Honey

Money is one of life's lessons that everyone learns at his or her own pace. Hands-on experience is probably the best way to teach children about money. If your children are too young to understand the values of coins and bills, they can still be taught that people need to earn money, save it, and know how to spend it wisely. The following activities teach basic money concepts. Follow up these activities with a trip to the candy store (candy is one of the few items you can still purchase with coins), giving each child coins of their own to spend.

Restaurant

MATERIALS: play money
magazines
scissors/glue/markers
paper plates and cups
paper

PREPARATION: Prepare a two-page menu by stapling two sheets of white paper together, using colored paper for covers.

ACTIVITY: Children cut meals from magazines and glue them to paper plates. On the menus, write down the meal and, using dollar increments, write a price for each meal (ie: spaghetti $2.00). Have them cut out beverages and desserts, as well as dinners. The children can decorate the covers of each menu.

When the meals are complete, appoint a waiter/waitress and customers. Give each customer a different amount of one dollar bills. The customers order their meals according to what they can afford. The waiter/waitress serves them and, after pretend eating, the customer must pay. Even infants can get involved in this role-playing by sitting in their high chairs and eating their make believe meals with an older child playing the part of a parent. Place school age children in strategic spots where they can help younger ones choose items from the menus. Those children learning to recognize numbers will be able to pay without assistance, but will need help reading the menu. Follow up the activity with discussions about nutrition and food groups.

ALL

CONCEPTS:
- ◆ money value
- ◆ counting/number recognition
- ◆ adding/subtracting
- ◆ social skills.
- ◆ role-playing

MATERIALS: empty food boxes
empty cans/containers
paper
marker
play cash register (optional)
shopping basket (optional)
play money
shopping bags

PREPARATION: Cut 2" x 2" squares of paper. Write dollar amounts on each. Next to the number amount, draw pictures of dollar bills to match. Attach prices to items of food or non-food containers. Set up a room or table to simulate the grocery store.

ACTIVITY: Children take turns being customers and clerks. Give each child money to spend and have them fill their baskets. Involve infants and toddlers in the role-playing by allowing them to pick items to buy from the store and having their role-playing "parents" pay for them. Clerks can count the money and bag the groceries. By using dollar bills only, no change will be involved.

CONCEPTS:
◆ money value
◆ counting
◆ number recognition
◆ adding
◆ social skills
◆ role-playing

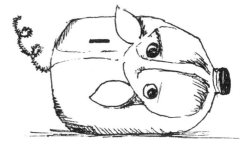

MATERIALS: milk cartons
play money
paint/brushes

ACTIVITY: The children decorate plastic milk cartons (or other containers, ie: shoe boxes, margarine tubs, dish-soap bottles, etc.) with paint. When dry, cut slits into the cartons to make piggy banks. Have children think of ways to earn "play money". Every time a child earns money, he or she drops it into the bank. At the end of each week, children add up their "play money" to see what they have earned. They return the money and begin again. Give out rewards for a certain amount of "money" earned.

If you are adventurous, put infants in a high chair with an art smock and, using an edible paint, let them finger paint their own banks.

 In toddlers' painted banks, make holes big enough to fit a cookie through. When a toddler accomplishes cooperation or other special deeds, let him or her put a cracker or cookie into the hole. At the end of the day, you can count the crackers or cookies together and the toddler can enjoy the reward.

 School age children could use real money and help younger children count.

CONCEPTS:
- ◆ math computation
- ◆ money value
- ◆ responsibility
- ◆ behavior modification

Plate Clocks

MATERIALS: paper/paper plates
pipe cleaners
posterboard
markers/glue/fasteners

PREPARATION: Write numbers 1-12 on 1" square paper. Draw hands of clock and birds on posterboard. Draw dots on the paper plates where the numbers will go. Cut the cuckoo door with a razor blade (have children keep their distance).

ACTIVITY: Children glue numbers next to the dots on the plate. Encourage children with writing abilities to write their own numbers on the squares. Cut hands of clock and attach with a fastener to the middle of the plate. Color and cut out the cuckoo birds. Staple one end of the pipe cleaner to the bird and the other end to the back of the plate behind the doors. Show the children different hours on the clock. Each time the hour hand is on a number, the children open their clock doors and say "cu-ckoo" as many times as the number says. Older kindergarten children can work with hours and half-hour increments.

CONCEPTS:
- ◆ counting/number recognition
- ◆ telling time
- ◆ hand/eye coordination
- ◆ fine motor skills

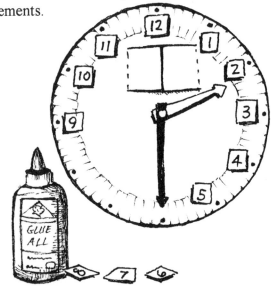

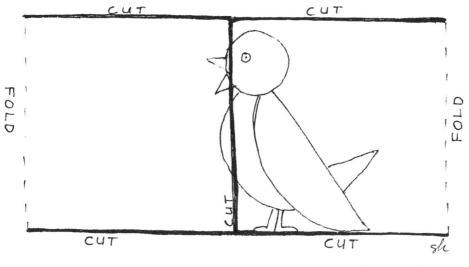

CUCKOO BIRD DOOR (SIZE)

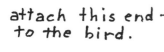
attach this end
to the bird.

attach this end
to the back of
the plate.

PIPE CLEANER

BIRD PATTERN

CLOCK HANDS PATTERN

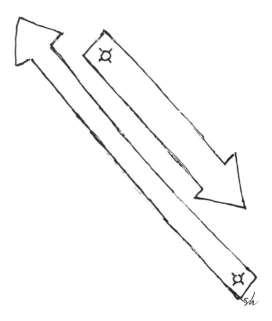

Make sure the bird is small enough for his door!

MATERIALS: 10 cardboard squares
tape
marker

PREPARATION: Write the numbers 1-10 on cardboard squares. In a hopscotch pattern, tape cardboard numbers to a bare floor.

ACTIVITY: Have children jump from one number to another in numerical order. Change the activity by calling out specific numbers or having children jump one-legged.

 Put infant on the floor and, each time the infant crawls on a number, ask your preschoolers and kindergartners to call out the number. The infant will feel like part of the group while the older children will have fun anticipating the next number.

 Instruct toddlers to hop from one square to another without worrying about number recognition. Make a set of picture, shape or color cards just for toddlers to use.

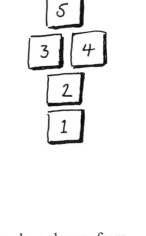

 School age children can use the hopscotch numbers to practice addition or multiplication. Have them jump on two different numbers with one foot on each and end with a jump with two feet on the answer or call out answers bigger than ten.

VARIATION: Play Table Hopscotch by making a hopscotch board, as shown, from cardboard squares. Set the squares onto the table and have the children try pitching pennies or beans onto the numbers. When one lands on a number, the children call out that number. Play a game where each child gets to pitch ten pennies and keep score by adding the numbers where the pennies or beans land.

MATERIALS: hangers
yarn
paper or light cardboard
scissors

PREPARATION: Draw shapes on paper or cardboard. Cut yarn into different lengths.

ACTIVITY: After the children cut out the shapes, ask each child to name each shape (or name the shape and have the child find it). Punch a hole at the top of that shape and let the children string their shapes. Tie one end of the yarn to the shape and the other end to the hanger. Continue the activity until all shapes are hung.

 Give infants the shapes to hold and examine. After the mobile is complete, hang it where the child can touch it, look at it, and even blow it around.

 Toddlers will need their shapes precut but can be taught shape names and will want to string their own shapes.

 Have school age children find more sophisticated shapes or build three-dimensional shapes (ie: cubes) to hang on their mobiles.

CONCEPTS:
- ◆ shape recognition
- ◆ fine motor skills

Chapter 5:

Scientifically Speaking-Science

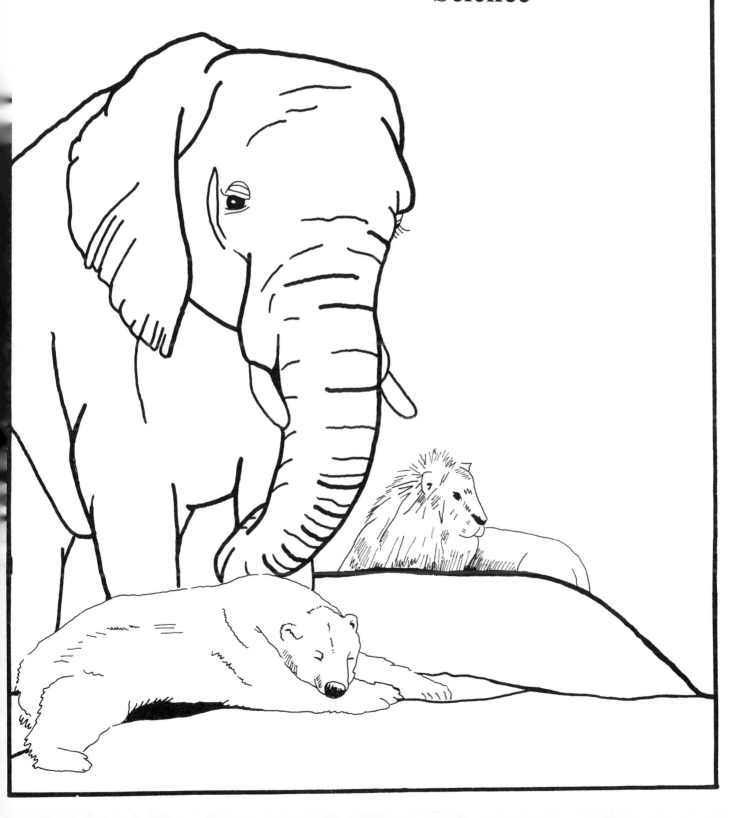

Chapter 5 Introduction

Science is a fascinating subject because it constantly surrounds us. Children are naturally inquisitive, a quality necessary and exciting in scientific exploration. Although we may not have the answers to all of their questions, exploring "hands on" experimenting and open discussions gives the child more exposure to how the world works. Infants and toddlers may not be asking the questions, but rest assured that they have already begun exploring the world around them. Preschoolers will bombard you with questions and school age children will love to offer their theories. The group of activities in this chapter just tips the iceberg of Science possibilities to use with children. Look around and explore with your children. Research more ways to introduce new concepts. Keep concepts simple, but always encourage questions.

MATERIALS: paper
pen
safety pins

PREPARATION: Draw a type of animal or fish on a piece of paper (or cut out pictures and glue to paper).

ACTIVITY: Pin a card on the back of each child so that they do not know which animal is on their card. Have the children go around to each other and ask questions about the animal that is pinned to their backs (example: "Where do I live?"). They can keep asking until they solve the mystery and guess the animal.

 After children have guessed their animals, show infants the pictures and say the animals' names.

 Toddlers can participate in this game after the guessing is complete. Have all the children form a line and ask the toddler to find each animal.

 Give older children cards with the animal names and have them match the name with the pictures.

CONCEPTS:
- problem-solving
- animal characteristics
- language development
- deduction

Changing Colors

MATERIALS: paper
leaf pattern (trace around several different leaves)
scissors
glue

PREPARATION: Draw a picture of a tree trunk with branches, roots, and the ground. On green, yellow, brown, red, and orange paper, use your leaf patterns to trace leaves.

ACTIVITY: Have a discussion about why the leaves change colors in the Fall. Explain that the green in leaves is called chlorophyll. With sunlight and water, the leaves make food for the tree by the process of photosynthesis. When the weather gets colder, no water gets to the leaf and the chlorophyll disappears. The leaves start dying and turning other colors until they are brown and break off. The children can then cut out their leaves and glue them on the branches or to the ground if the leaves have changed colors. Follow up the activity with a walk to collect different colored leaves. See if there is some green left on the leaves or if the leaves have completely changed.

 Pre-cut leaves and give to infants to hold and examine. Older infants can help find leaves during the walk. Help older infants put leaves on their pictures. Talk to them and reinforce the words "tree" and "leaf".

 Pre-cut leaves for toddlers. With help, toddlers can try cutting and gluing their leaves.

 School age children can find different types of leaves and trace patterns onto paper. See if they can name the type of tree from the shape of the leaf.

CONCEPTS:
- ◆ photosynthesis
- ◆ trees
- ◆ seasons
- ◆ problem-solving
- ◆ fine motor skills

Farm & Zoo

MATERIALS: animal, barn, and cage patterns
paper
glue
scissors

PREPARATION: Cut strips of black paper. Draw and cut red barn using rectangles and semi- circles. Make copies of animal patterns for each child.

ACTIVITY: Children glue pieces for the barn onto one sheet of paper. The zoo cages will be glued to another sheet. Talk about each animal (where they live, characteristics, names). The children color and cut their animals. Then instruct the children to glue the farm animals onto the paper with the barn and the zoo animals onto the paper with the zoo cages.

 Glue animal pictures onto the paper and cut each animal for infants. Laminate the animals and give them to the infant for playing and exploring. Name each animal.

 Cut animals ahead of time and assist toddlers in assembling barns and cages. They can decide where each animal lives and glue them to the appropriate home.

CONCEPTS:
- ◆ animal homes
- ◆ animal names
- ◆ problem-solving
- ◆ fine motor development

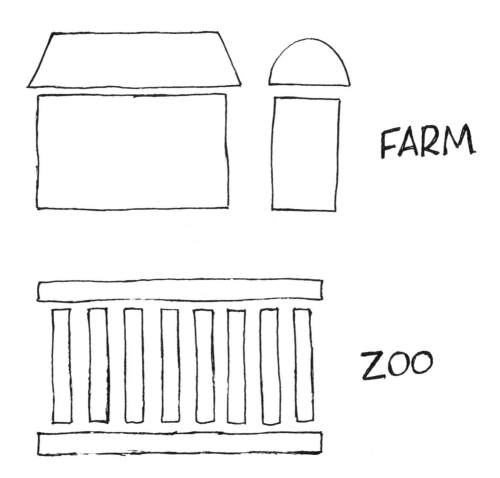

FARM

ZOO

Astro-Nomical

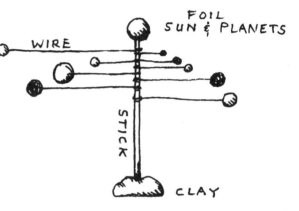

WIRE

FOIL
SUN & PLANETS

STICK

CLAY

MATERIALS: library book about the solar system
sturdy stick (between 12" - 15")
wire/foil
clay

PREPARATION: Cut nine pieces of wire into different lengths proportional to the distance of planets from the sun.

ACTIVITY: Show pictures of the planets rotating around the sun. Discuss how each planet revolves around the sun and how they rotate individually. Name the planets in order from the sun. Observe the largest to the smallest. Recreate the solar system. Insert stick into a lump of clay.

Wrap one end of each wire around the stick, leaving about an inch between each wire. Have the children wrap pieces of foil into little balls around the outside ends of each wire (making the balls larger for larger planets). They can form a large foil ball at the tip of the stick to represent the sun. Talk about the importance of the sun to the earth. Encourage questions and discussion.

Under **strict** supervision, infants and toddlers can experiment with touching and crushing foil pieces. Toddlers can compare big and little.

School age children can get more involved with this project by choosing a favorite planet to research. Have them share their information and drawings with the group. Write a story of what life would be like on that planet.

CONCEPTS:
- ◆ solar system
- ◆ rotation
- ◆ environment
- ◆ problem-solving
- ◆ size comparison

Order from Sun	Size from biggest to smallest
◆ Mercury	◆ Jupiter
◆ Venus	◆ Saturn
◆ Earth	◆ Uranus
◆ Mars	◆ Neptune
◆ Jupiter	◆ Earth
◆ Saturn	◆ Venus
◆ Uranus	◆ Mars
◆ Neptune/Pluto	◆ Pluto/Mercury

Dinosaur Eggs

MATERIALS: white and green paper
egg and baby dinosaur patterns
fasteners/tape
scissors

PREPARATION: Copy egg pattern on white construction paper. Copy baby dinosaur pattern on green construction paper, or white if you want the children to color their dinosaurs.

ACTIVITY: This activity is a good follow-up project to an animal unit on dinosaurs. Children cut out their eggs and dinosaurs. Tape pockets to the back of the bottom of the eggs. After punching holes where indicated in the diagram, fasten the two eggshells together. Children can put their baby dinosaurs in the pocket. They will delight in opening and closing the eggshells and will hatch and re-hatch their dinosaurs over and over again.

 Pre-cut eggs and dinosaurs for infants and toddlers. Let them color their own dinosaurs, put the fasteners in the holes, and play.

CONCEPTS:
- ◆ dinosaurs
- ◆ eggs
- ◆ fine motor development

VARIATION: For further study, teach the children about fossils. Pour craft plaster into pie tins and set objects (ie: seashells, leaves, bones, etc.) to make fossils. When the plaster dries, remove the object to see its imprint.
Visit a natural history museum to see dinosaur displays.

Fasten together at holes.

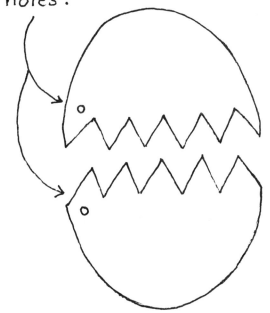

Tape a pocket to the back to keep baby dinosaur.

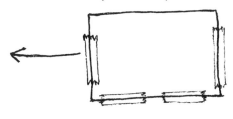

More Animal Studies

Types of animals and their characteristics and behaviors are always fun lessons for children. Study animals in groups or study one animal at a time. Plan to do an animal unit several times a month. The next step is to get a book from the library about that particular group or individual animal. Decide which basic ideas you want to teach the children (food, habitat, unusual behaviors or characteristics). When teaching each group, thumb through the book with the children, showing different pictures and names. Keep the lessons simple. Do a follow up activity, using some of the following ideas:

1. Silhouette animals in the group and have the children color, cut, and glue the outlines to paper. See how many animals they can recognize.
2. Choose one animal from the group and re-create that animal using clay, paper, paper plates, straws, or other craft material.
3. Choose an animal from the group to make into hand or finger puppets. Have children give a show.
4. Go on a field trip to the zoo and see how many animals the children can recognize from that group. Have them draw pictures of their favorite animal when they return from the trip.
5. Re-create habitats of animals from the group you are studying.
6. Have children or neighbors bring their pets to share for the day.
7. Find books about an animal from the group for storytelling.
8. Make worksheets with pictures of animals from the group and have the children name and color each animal.
9. Have children act out animal behaviors.
10. Make cookies shaped like animals.
11. Using dry food ingredients, make animal mosaics.
12. Create stories about animals.
13. Sing songs and rhymes about animals.

CONCEPTS:
- ◆ animal characteristics, behavior and habitat
- ◆ geographical locations of animals
- ◆ reading reinforcement through animal books
- ◆ creative dramatics/singing
- ◆ fine motor skills

SAMPLE ACTIVITIES AND PATTERNS:

RODENTS

Use the porcupine pattern to draw animal parts onto construction paper. For the porcupine, cut long triangles out of contrasting paper and have the children glue the needles in one direction.

PETS

Copy the pet worksheet and have children color the pets. Have each child dictate a story about their favorite pet. Ask children how they would take care of their pets.

AUSTRALIAN ANIMALS

After studying the marsupials of Australia, children fold a piece of gray paper in half. Trace the koala pattern, making sure the head is at the fold. Cut the animals from the doubled paper and they will stand up! The children can color or cut eyes, noses, eucalyptus leaves and other distinguishing features.

AFRICAN ANIMALS

Using paper plates and construction paper, have children make lions or elephants. Trace the ape mask pattern from tagboard. Have the children color, cut, and wear!

strip

cut contrasting colored strips; curl and glue.

Cut ears and trunk from construction paper.

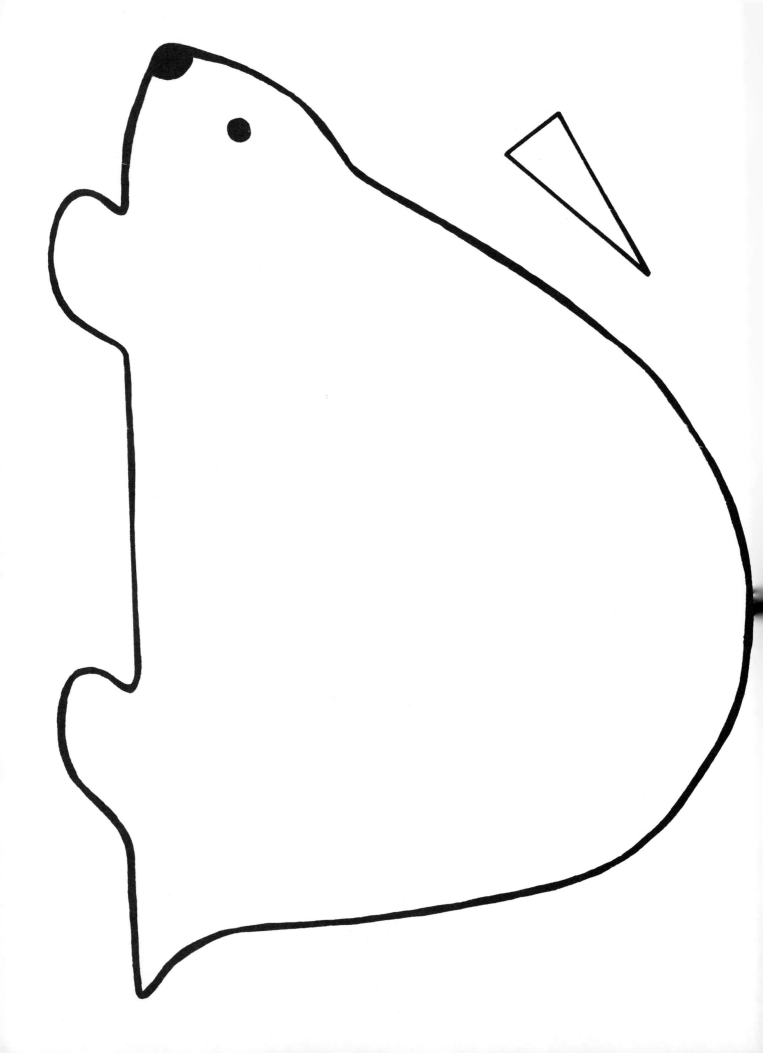

MATERIALS: magnets
objects (metallic and non metallic)

ACTIVITY: Place different objects in the middle of the floor and gather the children around the objects. Show the children how the magnet sticks to metal objects. Children take turns guessing which objects the magnet will attract and which ones will not attract. Encourage discussion after the guessing game.

CONCEPTS:
- ◆ magnets
- ◆ deduction
- ◆ problem-solving

VARIATION:
Buy metal scraps or magnet kits. Pour scraps into a shoebox lid. Let the children experiment and draw pictures by moving their magnet under the lid.

MATERIALS: yarn
big construction paper/scrap colored paper
contact paper
crepe paper streamers
string
scissors
glue/tape

ACTIVITY: Curve and tape big construction paper into cylinder shape. Children can cut shapes or pictures from scrap colored paper and glue onto the large construction paper before making their cylinders. Glue strips of crepe paper streamers to the inside of the bottom opening of the cylinder. Staple string for hanging to the top section of the wind sock.
(note: If you wish to laminate these, do it before taping the cylinder).

 If your infant is old enough to hold a crayon, put the construction paper on the floor and let the scribbling begin! After you put the wind sock together, take the child with you outside to hang it up and watch it blow in the wind.

Toddlers will need help attaching their streamers. After the wind socks are complete, your toddler will delight in running around outside carrying the wind sock in the breeze.

 After the wind socks are completed, school age children can make a daily chart and keep track of the wind direction for the week.

CONCEPTS:
- ◆ weather
- ◆ fine motor skills
- ◆ creativity

Making Peanut Butter

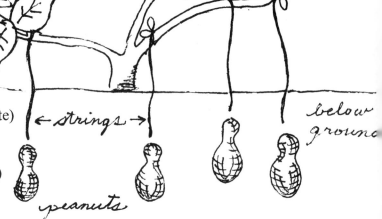

← strings →

below ground

peanuts

MATERIALS: paper(green/brown/white)
marker/ string
large bag of peanuts
vegetable oil (1-2 Tbsp)
salt

PREPARATION: Get a book from the library about peanuts. Draw a line horizontally on the white paper. Above the line, draw twigs as shown in the following diagram.

ACTIVITY: Read about peanuts to the children. Learn how and where they grow and how they are used. Teach them the nutritional value. With markers, the children can draw pictures of peanuts on brown paper and cut them out. Glue strings from the twigs to below the line. Children can glue their peanuts to the bottom end of the string to show how peanuts grow underground. After the lesson, children can shell the peanuts and put them into the blender with oil and salt. Blend mixture until smooth. Serve on bananas, bread, celery sticks, or crackers.

 Draw and cut toddlers' paper peanuts for them to glue. Keep a <u>careful</u> watch while they help shell the peanuts.

 School age children can research how to grow peanuts at home.

CONCEPTS:
- ◆ peanuts
- ◆ horticulture
- ◆ nutrition
- ◆ fine motor skills

optional numbers

VARIATIONS: For a Math activity, number pictures of peanuts to match vines going into the ground. Children can count and put numbered peanuts in order. For a History lesson, have them read about George Washington Carver, who invented hundreds of ways to use peanuts.

MATERIALS: paper
yarn
wire/hanger
markers
scissors

PREPARATION:
On white paper, draw rainbows, wind, clouds, raindrops, suns, and snowflakes.

ACTIVITY: Talk about different kinds of weather. Discuss what causes rain, clouds, rainbows, snow, and wind. Have the children color and cut out the weather pictures. Staple yarn to the pictures and tie them to the bent wire.

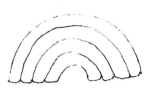

 Pre-cut pictures for toddlers and have them color.

In addition to the activity, school age children can keep a chart of the daily weather report.

CONCEPTS:
- ◆ environment
- ◆ weather
- ◆ fine motor development
- ◆ problem-solving
- ◆ charting
- ◆ language skills

MATERIALS: cotton balls
paper

glue
marker
cherries

PREPARATION: Draw a tree on paper.

ACTIVITY: Children glue cotton balls to the trees to simulate cherry blossoms.
Discuss fruit trees that blossom. Cut cherries in half and blot the juicy part onto the tree to leave prints looking like cherries. Take a drive in the Spring and observe different fruit trees in bloom.

ALL

CONCEPTS:
- ◆ trees
- ◆ fruit
- ◆ fine motor development

VARIATIONS: Bake a cherry cobbler with the children for a Nutrition project.

MATERIALS: large pieces of newsprint (or roll paper)
crayons
scissors
vital organs patterns

ACTIVITY: Children lie on the sheet of paper. With a crayon, have children trace around each other's bodies. Discuss different parts of the outside appearance of the toes and ears. Name different parts of the body (arms, neck, legs, head, skin, etc.) and let children point to those parts. Discuss what each body part can do and its purpose.

CONCEPTS:
- ◆ body and functions
- ◆ self-awareness
- ◆ fine motor development

VARIATION: Preschoolers and school age children can explore the inside of the body. Trace the following vital organ patterns and discuss the function of each organ (use a book from the library to brush up on functions and show pictures to the children). The children can cut out the organs and glue them to their outlines of themselves.

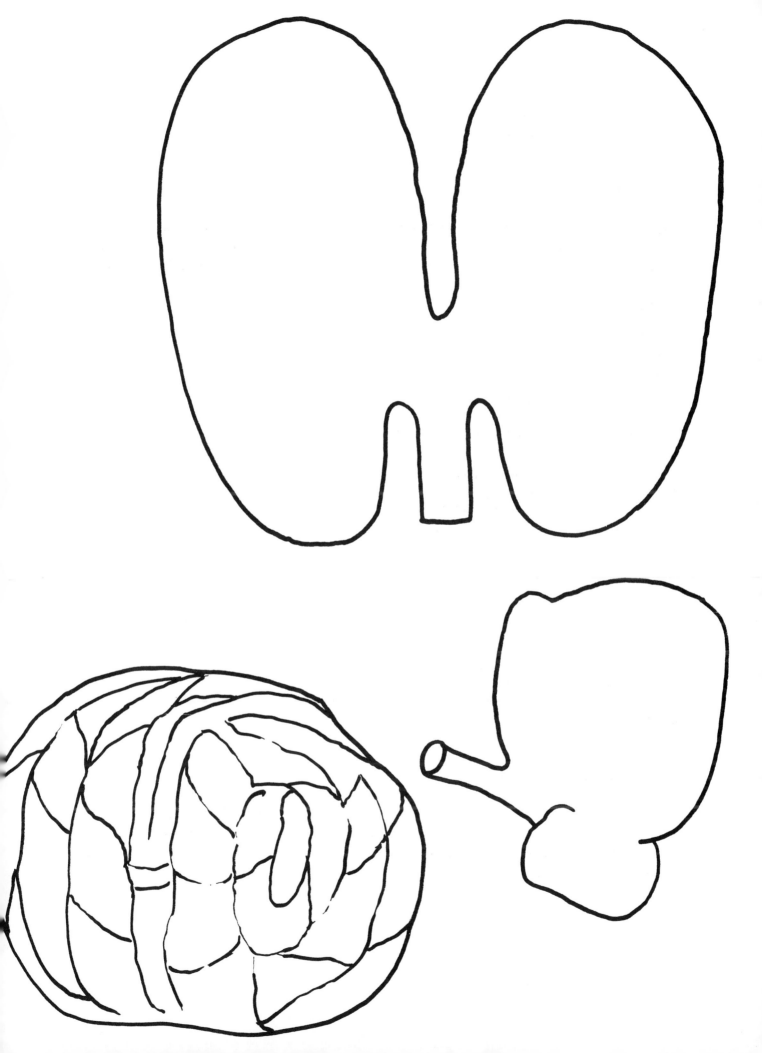

MATERIALS: plastic sandwich bags
items with distinctive odors:
(vanilla, onions, maple syrup, vinegar)
items with distinctive tastes:
(dill pickles, grapefruit, sugar, honey, coconut, chocolate chips)
tape player
large cardboard box
scissors
paper/paint/yarn
items with distinctive texture:
(smooth rocks, rough wood, ice cubes, cotton balls, sandpaper)

ACTIVITY: Have a discussion about the five senses. Tell the children they will be learning about a different sense every day for five days (or one day a week for five weeks).

Hearing:

Prerecord sounds on a tape player. Record hammering, sneezing, singing, coughing, birds, whistling, vacuum cleaner, trickling water, and any other sounds you think the children can recognize. Gather children in a circle and have them close their eyes. See how many sounds they can recognize. Discuss the importance of hearing and what life would be like without it.

Smelling:

Put odoriforous items into plastic sandwich bags. With their eyes closed, have children pass one bag at a time under their noses and guess the smell. Discuss favorite and least favorite odors.

Tasting:

Put tasting items into plastic sandwich bags. Blindfold one child at a time for each taste test. Have the child taste the item and describe the taste to the other children. The other children can see what the blindfolded child is tasting and will tell whether that child has guessed correctly.

Seeing:

Sit in a circle on the floor. Start a guessing game with a description of something in the room ("I see something round, red, and big"). Continue with a few more examples and then allow the child who guesses correctly to be the "describer".

Touching:

Cut a round hole in a cardboard box for a mouth. Have the children decorate it with hair, eyes, ears and nose. Put distinctive feeling items into the box. Each child can have a turn to reach into the box and feel one item. Encourage them to describe the item (cold, smooth, rough, bumpy) so the other children can guess. If the others cannot guess, have the child feeling guess and show the item to the group. The children can play with the "feely" box after the activity is completed.

Follow up each of the senses with a worksheet to reinforce what the children have learned. When all the senses have been covered, have a review day. Gather different items and ask the children which senses can be used to recognize those items. Be sure to ask questions like: "If you could not see the table, what other ways would help you know it is a table"? Answers will range from "Someone tells me" (hearing) to "Licking the table" (tasting). Ask which is the "best" way to recognize the objects that are named. Follow up this activity with a final worksheet.

ALL: All the children will enjoy participating in these activities, although infants will be unable to join in the discussions and worksheets.

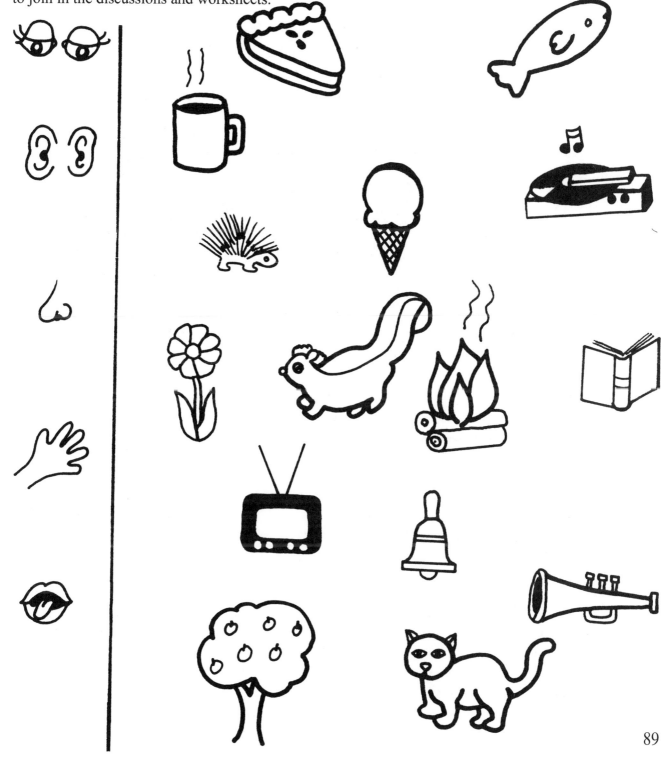

MATERIALS: Egg cartons (individual cups separated) or Styrofoam cups
potting soil
spoons
seeds (fruit, vegetable, flower)
paper
marker
pebbles

PREPARATION: Make a chart with the seed names on the left hand side and the days across the top.

ACTIVITY: Have children put a few pebbles at the bottom of their cups for drainage. Fill the cups with potting soil and plant the seeds in the top of the soil according to the package specifications. Let the children water their seeds and place them in a window. Discuss the different types of seeds they planted (vegetable, fruit, grass). Have them guess which seeds will grow the fastest and slowest. Mark their guesses on a separate piece of paper. For four weeks, have the children check their plants daily. When the plants begin to grow, help them measure the growth and

write it on the chart. At the end of four weeks, discuss the growth with the children and see how many of them guessed correctly. If you have room in your yard for a garden, transplant the plants with the children and observe the results.

 Infants and toddlers can join in the planting and observe the growth of the plants.

Leave the measuring and graphing to the preschoolers and older children.

CONCEPTS:
  ◆ plant variations
  ◆ plant survival
  ◆ measurement
  ◆ charts
  ◆ problem-solving
  ◆ deduction

VARIATION: Use this activity as a Nutrition project by discussing the different food groups and which plants fall into those groups. Measuring/ graphs can reinforce Math lessons.

MATERIALS: pan
ruler
marker/crayons
paper
glue

PREPARATION: On paper, draw clouds, raindrops, and ovals for ponds.

ACTIVITY: Children are always asking questions about water. "How do we get water?" and "Why does it rain?" are popular questions. Discuss "evaporation" with the children. Have the children cut out raindrops, ponds and clouds. On one cloud, color the bottom half dark (using gray, black or blue crayons). Explain how the water drops rise and cling to dust particles to form the beginning of the cloud. As more droplets rise, the cloud gets bigger and darker until it is too heavy and it falls to the ground as rain. The children can illustrate this concept by gluing their pictures to the paper to show how evaporation works. After the pictures are completed, fill a pan with water, measure the water level and set the pan outdoors. Check and measure the water daily so the children can see the decreasing water level. Ask open ended questions about ways the water gets to our homes, how to conserve water, and how to keep water clean.

CONCEPTS:
- ◆ evaporation
- ◆ weather
- ◆ conservation
- ◆ problem-solving

VARIATION: This activity can also be used as a Math unit to reinforce measuring.

MATERIALS: collect twigs, leaves, and mud
bird patterns (next page)
cardboard (8" x 10") paper
scissors
crayons
play dough
glue

PREPARATION: Copy the bird patterns onto paper.

ACTIVITY: Take a nature hike with all of the children to observe birds. Collect twigs and leaves to make nests. Discuss birds and their habits. On the piece of cardboard, children can construct nests by using mud, twigs, and leaves (be sure the work area is well protected). While the nests dry, have the children form eggs from the play dough. Later, they can put their homemade eggs into their nests. Follow up the activity with the coloring and cutting of their bird pictures. Have children name each bird.

 Infants and toddlers will enjoy mud painting on their cardboard. Put them in a highchair if necessary, dress them in smocks, and watch them closely so the mud goes on the cardboard and not into their mouths.

 School age children would enjoy researching types of birds and their eggs. Have children try molding and painting eggs to match different types of birds (check out a book from the library).

CONCEPTS:
- ◆ birds
- ◆ creativity
- ◆ fine motor skills
- ◆ observation

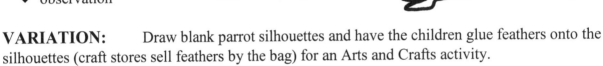

VARIATION: Draw blank parrot silhouettes and have the children glue feathers onto the silhouettes (craft stores sell feathers by the bag) for an Arts and Crafts activity.

92

Snails

MATERIALS: egg cartons
light cardboard
pipe cleaners
paper
scissors/glue
crayons/paint (optional)

PREPARATION: Draw circles on 6" x 6" cardboard. Cut egg cartons into three sections. Draw sets of eyes from paper (or buy craft eyes). Make slits in the tops of the egg carton sections. Find information about snails in an encyclopedia or library book.

ACTIVITY: Children cut out circles and eyes. They can color or paint the circles and insert them into the slits of the egg cartons. Have them glue the eyes on the front of the egg carton section. Fold pipe cleaner in half and curl the ends. Poke a hole in the head of the snail and insert the folded end of the pipe cleaner. Discuss snail behavior and habitats.

 Show your infant a completed snail. Let them feel and examine it under supervision.

 Precut everything for toddlers. Direct gluing and help them insert the shells and antennae. Let them color or paint their shells.

 School age children would be very interested in recreating a real habitat for snails. Have them use an old jar, fish bowl, or fish tank. Take them to the pet store to inquire about the care of snails. They could even purchase one with their own money (or find one under rotting leaves in the backyard), keep it as a pet, and have the younger children observe.

CONCEPTS:
- ◆ animal behavior
- ◆ shapes
- ◆ hand-eye coordination
- ◆ fine motor skills

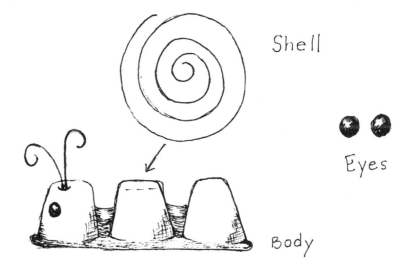

Shell

Eyes

Body

MATERIALS: jars with lids
vegetable oil
water
blue food color
play dough
waterproof varnish or seal

ACTIVITY: **Day 1:** Children model sea creatures (ie: octopus, seahorse, fish, sharks). Bake creatures in oven at 200 degrees until firm. When cooled, spray or brush on water sealant and let dry.

Day 2. Have the children pour oil into jars with a touch of water and food coloring. They can put their creatures in the jar and cover.

 Toddlers will need assistance, but can easily participate in the activity.

School age children can write stories about their ocean jars.

CONCEPTS:
- ◆ ocean life
- ◆ fine motor skills
- ◆ environmental study
- ◆ creativity

VARIATIONS: After studying about ocean creatures, children draw (using crayons) pictures of their favorite sea animals. The children brush over their pictures with blue and green watercolors to create a watery effect.

OCEAN CREATURE SILHOUETTES

Use the following patterns to trace ocean animals onto black construction paper. Children cut out the silhouettes and glue onto blue construction paper. Add other ocean life to the scene. Have the children name the animals according to their shapes.

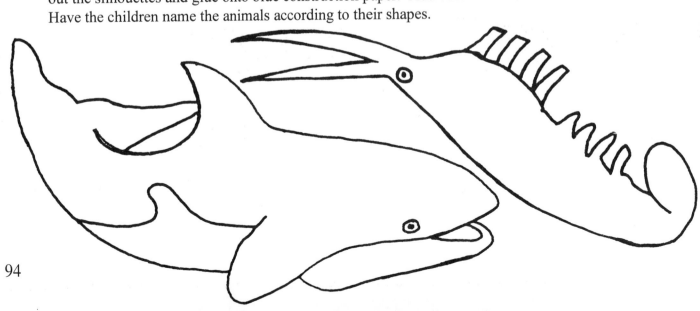

94

CHAPTER 6:

PAST, PRESENT,
& FUTURE-
SOCIAL STUDIES

CHAPTER 6 Introduction

Social Studies cover a variety of topics with many activity possibilities. The key to Social Studies topics at a preschool level is to keep lessons simple, just touching on facts that will make some impression and expose children to the world around them. Preschoolers and younger children are in their own little worlds, so begin a Social Studies curriculum around that world. Start your program with activities such as; me, family, neighborhood, transportation, and feelings. Then expand to other areas, like major historical events, geography, and cultural studies. This chapter will give you some ideas on simplifying concepts and creating your own activities.

MATERIALS: paper
       scissors
       glue
       markers

PREPARATION: Write the words "My Favorites" at the top of the paper. On the left hand side of the paper, write these suggestions:

• books	• toys	• movies
• TV show	• food	• friends
• clothes	• songs	• vacation
• games	• neighbors	• character
• animals	• things to do	• treats
• cartoon	with my family	
	• desserts	

ACTIVITY: Gather the group together and read the list to the children. Have them think about the list. On a separate piece of paper, the children can draw or cut magazine pictures and glue their favorite things. While the children are busy creating their pictures, interview each child and write their answers next to the words you have prepared on the other paper.

 Look through magazines with your infants and toddlers. Find any pictures that you know they like and cut them out. Toddlers can glue them to their papers while you name the pictures.

 Have school age children write small paragraphs next to the words you have written on their papers. Encourage them to give reasons why the items they have chosen are their favorites.

MATERIALS: paper/markers
                   construction paper
                   hole punch
                   fasteners
                   mirrors

PREPARATION: Make booklets with construction paper covers. Fasten together at the top left hand corner with fastener.

ACTIVITY: In a group discussion, encourage children to discuss things about themselves. Some suggestions for discussion are:

1. Describe how you look.
2. Name two things you feel you can do well.
3. Tell about your family.
4. What kinds of responsibilities do you have at home?
5. What do you like about your room?
6. If you could change one thing about yourself, what would it be?
7. How can you help where you live be a better place?
8. What kinds of things do you enjoy doing by yourself?
9. Where do you live? Do you know your phone number?

After discussion, have the children study themselves in a mirror and, on the first page of their booklets, draw a picture of themselves. Encourage children to draw pictures in their booklets about the things they have discussed. This would be a good time to teach them their addresses and phone numbers. Write them in their booklets. From magazines, children can cut and paste pictures that describe themselves. Share the booklets with each other.

 Children cut words from magazines to describe some of their answers. Have the children write autobiographies and share them with everyone.

CONCEPTS:
◆ self-awareness
◆ social development
◆ descriptive vocabulary
◆ creativity
◆ problem-solving

MATERIALS: magazines
paper
glue/scissors
paper plates
file folders

PREPARATION: Cut pictures from magazines of people showing different expressions and feelings. Mark each file folder with a word describing a different feeling (beside the word, draw a face that describes that feeling).

ACTIVITY: Lay all the cutout pictures on the floor and have children group around the pictures. Show the children each file folder separately and encourage discussion. Ask what kinds of situations make them feel like the people in the pictures. Have the children take turns finding pictures of people that show those feelings and let them cut the pictures inside the folder. Finish the activity with the children cutting one picture from a magazine that describes how they are feeling. Glue the picture to a paper plate with their name.

 Show infants pictures and describe the pictures to them. Give them a paper plate with a picture to examine.

 Toddlers will enjoy participating in the matching of feelings to the folders. Assist them in finding pictures for their plates.

 Children can write a list of as many words as they can think of to describe different feelings.

CONCEPTS:
- ◆ nonverbal communication
- ◆ picture recognition
- ◆ descriptive vocabulary
- ◆ feelings
- ◆ self-awareness
- ◆ matching

MATERIALS: milk cartons
paint
paper
scissors/glue

ACTIVITY: With the children, discuss what kinds of things are found in a village, town, or city. Each child chooses a milk carton to paint and design into a building. Use paper to make windows, signs, chimneys and other accessories. When the buildings are completed, have fun arranging the village on a tabletop or in a sandbox. The children can use cars, trucks, little people and other play items with their villages.

 Involve infants in the playing process.

 Toddlers can paint and play. Help them decorate their buildings with paper.

Older children can make signs, 3-dimensional trees and other sophisticated additions to the village.

CONCEPTS:
- ◆ creative thinking
- ◆ problem-solving
- ◆ social structures

New News

MATERIALS: newspapers
paper
scissors/glue

ACTIVITY: Let children look through a newspaper. Encourage them to ask questions. Show the children different sections of the newspaper and discuss the importance of newspapers. Allow children to cut out pictures, words, and articles from the paper. Arrange onto paper to make their own mini papers.

 Help children write articles, interview people, draw pictures, and make a paper of their own.

CONCEPTS:
- ◆ newspaper awareness
- ◆ reading skills
- ◆ current events
- ◆ group discussion

VARIATION: Visit a local newspaper and learn how it operates.

MATERIALS: colored construction paper
magazines
scissors/glue

PREPARATION: Cut out triangles, squares, circles, and rectangles of all sizes and colors.

ACTIVITY: Explain to the children the meaning of transportation. Have an open discussion to see how many types of transportation they can name. With the shapes, the children can build some of these ideas. Use magazines to find additional transportation pictures.

 Older infants can play with the shapes and examine the pictures. Name each picture for them.

 Toddlers can look for pictures in magazines. They will need help building with shapes.

 Let the older children read stories related to types of transportation. Encourage them to design a new "type" of transportation using any available materials.

CONCEPTS:
◆ transportation
◆ creative thinking
◆ problem-solving
◆ vocabulary building

VARIATION: Take a field trip to an airport, train station, bus depot, or marina. Write stories about the experience for Reading. Have children set up their own pretend plane trip or train ride and role-play for Creative Dramatics.

MATERIALS: milk cartons
red/black paint
3" cardboard circles
black paper
red craft balls
glue

PREPARATION: Cut 3" cardboard circles. Cut strips of black paper to build ladders and rectangles for windows.

ACTIVITY: Talk about fire prevention. Ask questions about the cause of fires and ways fires can be avoided. Ask what firefighters do. To make fire trucks have children paint milk cartons red and the cardboard circles black. Glue rectangles for windows and strips of black paper for ladders. Use red pompons (or dyed cotton balls) for sirens. Finish the activity with a trip to a fire station. Have a practice fire drill.

ALL: Older infants can play with milk cartons. All others will participate in the entire activity.

CONCEPTS:
- fire prevention/ fire fighters
- safety awareness
- problem-solving
- fine motor skills

Traffic Lights

MATERIALS: paper (brown, red, green, yellow) scissors, glue

PREPARATION: Draw a traffic light on brown paper. Cut circles from the red, green, and yellow paper.

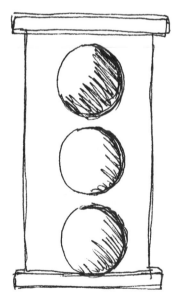

ACTIVITY: Teach the children what the colors on the stoplight represent. Have them cut out the stop lights and glue colored circles in stop light order. Play a game of "Red Light-Green Light". Have children stand next to each other in a straight line. Shouting "green light" allows them to move forward. Shout "red light" and they stop walking. Send traffic "offenders" back to the beginning. Have children take turns being the traffic light. Conclude activity by discussing traffic rules and their importance.

CONCEPTS:
- color differentiation
- traffic rules
- self-discipline
- large motor skills

MATERIALS: household materials (yarn, buttons, lids, cloth, Styrofoam, macaroni, etc.)
cardboard or posterboard
glue/markers

ACTIVITY: Talk about families. Discuss what makes a family, who is in a family, where families live, and why families are important. Set out a variety of household materials and let the children create pictures on cardboard of the people in their family.

 Put glue on the cardboard. Have older infants and toddlers put any materials on the glue to create a collage.

After portraits are finished, have children write a short story about their families.

CONCEPTS:
- ◆ family structures
- ◆ creative thinking skills
- ◆ fine motor skills

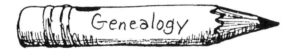

MATERIALS: paper
pencils
markers
family photographs

ACTIVITY: Have children study their family's history. Discuss what makes a family. Draw trees on paper and glue pictures of the family onto the trees

 Show your infants pictures of people in their family and name each person.

 Toddlers will be able to glue their pictures. Ask the children to name each person.

Have children interview their grandparents. Write stories about their grandparents' lives. Encourage them to find names as far back as possible and write a family tree.

CONCEPTS:
- ◆ family
- ◆ family history
- ◆ creative writing
- ◆ picture recognition

ALL: Take the children on a walk through the neighborhood. Take paper and pencils to jot down notes and make a map. Include houses, schools, parks, stores, and other landmarks. Let the younger children dictate to you anything that they notice about the neighborhood.

On their return home, give the children paper and crayons to draw pictures of things they saw along the way. Let them dictate comments to you about each picture and write those comments next to the pictures. Older children can do their own writing. When all the pictures are finished, put them into one booklet and make a cover. Call the book "Our Neighborhood". Discuss likes and dislikes of the neighborhood.

After careful study of your neighborhood, follow the drawn maps and, with the children, decide what should be included to make a diorama.

MATERIALS: variety of sizes of milk cartons
large cardboard (as large as desired for the entire neighborhood)
paint
paper
glue/scissors
sand
green rodent shavings (buy at pet store)

ACTIVITY: This activity can be an ongoing process because it is very detailed. Have children cut windows and doors out of small milk cartons. Paint and decorate. Make roofs from construction paper and attach with glue. The following materials can be used to construct specific items in the diorama.

1. trees/bushes - Either buy these in a hobby store or draw and cut them from cardboard.
2. roads - Glue and sprinkle sand or use black paint right on the cardboard.
3. stores - Use larger milk cartons and paint imitation store fronts.
4. stop signs - Buy these items in a hobby store or make them from cardboard.
5. grassy areas - Glue and sprinkle green rodent chips (found in pet stores).
6. other - Children can use their imaginations to make additional details from scraps, cardboard, string, and other materials.

MATERIALS: telephone book
paper
pencils

PREPARATION: Write a list of problems that children can solve by using the telephone book. Following are a few ideas to get started:

1. You want to buy a toy.
2. You have a toothache.
3. Your car needs new tires.
4. You want to buy a pet.
5. A house is on fire.
6. The sink is leaking.
7. The dog is sick.
8. The newspaper was not delivered.
9. Someone is hurt and needs an ambulance.
10. You want to call a friend but do not have the number.

ACTIVITY: Discuss the importance of the telephone book. Show the children the book and talk about the white and yellow pages. Read some of the headings. Read each problem to the children and have them discuss their ideas. Using a toy phone, simulate dialing phone numbers and talking to the person who will solve the problem.

Older infants and toddlers will have fun playing make believe phone calls. Give them specific people to call and encourage a pretend conversation.

In the yellow pages, have the children find advertisements that will solve each problem on the list.

CONCEPTS:
- social skills
- problem-solving
- alphabetizing

VARIATION: For younger children, cut advertisements from magazines and children can guess what the advertisement is selling.

MATERIALS: magazines
paper
scissors
glue

ACTIVITY: Group the children into a circle. Ask them questions about different feelings and give each child turns to participate in the discussion. Ask what makes them feel certain ways, why they feel that way, and how they deal with those feelings. Some feelings that can be discussed are anger, fear, sadness, happiness, and funniness. Have the children find pictures in the magazines that show some of these feelings. Cut and glue onto paper.

Precut pictures to show infants and toddlers.

After cutting the feelings pictures, the children can write captions beneath each picture.

CONCEPTS:
 ◆ communication skills
 ◆ self-awareness
 ◆ discipline
 ◆ social skills
 ◆ creative thought

ACTIVITY: In front of the group, interview one of the children (ask her questions about herself). After the children have seen how to interview another person, put the children into pairs so they can conduct their own interviews. Here are a few questions to help get started:

1. What do you like to play?
2. What is your favorite food?
3. How many people are in your family? What are their names?
4. What do you look like?
5. What special things does your family like to do?
6. What is your favorite movie?

When the interviews are completed, each child dictates to you what they have learned about the other person. Have them draw portraits of that person to attach with their biographies.

Older children can take notes while interviewing and write a biography on that person. Make book covers using cardboard and patterned contact paper. The children can find a biography of a famous person at the library to read and share.

CONCEPTS:
- ◆ social development
- ◆ biographies
- ◆ interviewing
- ◆ creativity

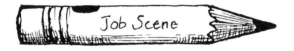

MATERIAL: magazines
library books about occupations
colored paper
scissors
glue

ACTIVITY: Read picture books from the library about types of occupations. Find pictures in magazines of people working at different types of jobs. Have children cut and glue the pictures and make collages. Name and discuss each occupation. Think of other occupations. Children can share their ideas about what they would like to be when they become adults. Follow up the discussion by making occupational hats (ie. nurses, policeman, fireman, baker).

 Name pictures of the people to the children. See if they can repeat the name. Ask the children to point to the "fireman", "doctor", etc.

 After school age children have decided what occupations interest them, have them do research to discover information about that career. Encourage them to find out what the person does, what kind of training or school is involved, and have them interview someone in that field to find out personal opinions.

CONCEPTS:
- ◆ social development
- ◆ employment/career responsibility
- ◆ language development
- ◆ problem-solving
- ◆ picture recognition
- ◆ vocabulary building

MATERIALS: magazine pictures (people, animals, objects)
manila file folders
glue/ scissors

PREPARATION: Glue a picture inside a manila folder. Cut a small square in the front of the folder (large enough to reveal a portion of the picture- cut additional holes as needed).

ACTIVITY: Children try to guess what the picture is inside the folder by looking under the tab. The children can make predictions and discuss the pictures. If the picture cannot be identified, cut more holes one at a time. Open the folder and see who was right (or close).

CONCEPTS:
- ◆ social development
- ◆ vocabulary building
- ◆ discrimination skills
- ◆ stimulates verbalization and description

MATERIALS: toothpicks
marshmallows

ACTIVITY: By using toothpicks and marshmallows as manipulatives, children problem-solve some of the following activities:

1. Think of different types of transportation. Design a new type of transportation or build a car, truck, or boat.
2. Create a playground, build a house, or design a school.
3. Make a model of yourself or your family.
4. Build something that is in your neighborhood.

Children can share each creation with the other children. Then they eat their marshmallows!

 Toddlers can practice their fine motor skills by building with the marshmallows and toothpicks.   **<u>Be sure to supervise them closely.</u>**

 Children can think of five words that begin or end with each letter in MARSHMALLOW (or five words found within the word itself- for example, RASH). Write a creative story with these words. Encourage older school age children to look in the dictionary for unfamiliar words to use in their stories.

CONCEPTS:
- ◆ creative thought
- ◆ social development
- ◆ building
- ◆ fine motor skills
- ◆ vocabulary building

VARIATIONS: Using toothpicks and marshmallows, build storybook characters or letters for Reading. Clocks, number lines, and shapes can be made for reinforcing Math concepts. Make animals for Science activities.

MATERIALS: book about Johnny Appleseed
posterboard/paper
green tissue paper
scissors/glue
marker

PREPARATION: Draw outlines of trees. Cut enough one inch squares of tissue paper to cover each tree.

ACTIVITY: Read stories about Johnny Appleseed. Have children glue leaf sections of trees and cover with tissue paper squares. Cut apples and glue to the trees. When the trees are complete, laminate, then cut them into puzzle pieces. Allow children time to assemble puzzles.

CONCEPTS:
- ◆ apples
- ◆ history of Johnny Appleseed
- ◆ fine motor skills

VARIATION: Find an apple tree and pick apples. For a Science activity, cut open an apple and examine it; discuss how the tree grows; and plant the seeds. Count seeds for a Math activity. Discuss apple dishes for Nutrition (try cooking something together). Cut apples cut in half, dip cut side in paint, and press onto paper to make apple star prints for Arts and Crafts.

APPLE PATTERNS

Native American cultures are not only fascinating for children, but have many activity possibilities. Get books and stories from the library to read and show pictures. Keep information simple and highlight major interests, such as homes, dress, lifestyles, and basic geographic areas.

MATERIALS: paper
toothpicks
clay
scissors/ glue

PREPARATION: Using teepee pattern, draw teepees on paper.

ACTIVITY: Children cut teepees, fold into a cone shape, and staple. Using colored paper, encourage children to cut and glue designs onto their teepees. Fold open the flaps. Stick toothpicks into two sides of a one-inch ball of clay. Poke each toothpick end through the top of the teepee. Vertically poke more toothpicks into the clay to resemble the poles of the teepee. Follow up the activity by using the worksheet of home dwellings. Ask the children which home would be the most fun place to live and why.

Toddlers can decorate teepees. If supervised, they can put toothpicks in the clay.

Children research Native American symbols and patterns to use as designs on their teepees. Have them explain the meanings of the symbols to the rest of the children.

CONCEPTS:
◆ Native American culture and dwellings
◆ fine motor development
◆ creative thinking

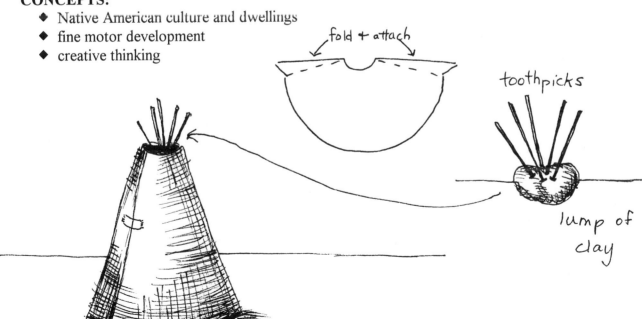

Pottery

MATERIALS: plastic containers (any shape)
papier mache paste
newspapers
paint

PREPARATION: Pre-cut plastic containers to look like vases, bowls, and pots (prepare work area for a mess). Strip newspapers. Prepare paste.

ACTIVITY: Have children cover containers with newspaper strips and paste using papier mache recipe in Chapter 2. Let pottery dry at least 24 hours. Have children paint designs with paint on the containers.

 Give your infant a paper bag full of newspaper strips to explore (be sure to supervise carefully). They can examine a dry, finished product, too.

Help toddlers along, but let them try the papier mache and painting.

Older children can make their own symbols and designs and write a story about the meaning of those symbols.

CONCEPTS:
- Native American culture and pottery
- color and design
- symbols
- storytelling
- fine motor development

Masks

MATERIALS: papier mache paste
newspapers
waxed paper
paints
tape
razor knife/scissors

PREPARATION: Tear enough newspaper strips to cover as many masks as necessary. Make papier mache paste from the recipe in Chapter 2.

ACTIVITY: Have children crumple about three sheets of newspapers and place onto the table in a face shape. Cover form with waxed paper. Tape the edges of the waxed paper to the table. Papier mache' the entire surface of the waxed paper and let dry. Pull up the mask form and cut into finished mask shapes. Cut eye holes, if desired. Children can paint their masks. Use yarn, beads, or other materials for additional decoration. Have a discussion about the significance of masks in Native American life. Compare those significances with the way masks are used today.

ALL: Everyone can participate in making these masks.

 Infants can explore newspaper strips and wear finished masks. From a high chair and with assistance, some older infants may even be able to put pasted strips onto the mask form.

CONCEPTS
- ◆ Native American culture
- ◆ masks and significance
- ◆ design
- ◆ fine motor development

MATERIALS: paint
colored paper
oatmeal cans
scissors/glue

ACTIVITY: Have each child design and paint a face on an oatmeal can. When each face is completed and dried, try building totem poles with all the cans.

 Infants will enjoy stacking the cans.

 Toddlers can paint the background, but will need faces painted for them.

Children can add wings, symmetrical designs, symbols, or even papier mache noses and other three-dimensional items. Give a Native American name to each face and write stories about the Native Americans whom each face represents.

CONCEPTS:
- ◆ Native American culture
- ◆ significance and structure of totem poles
- ◆ symmetry
- ◆ design
- ◆ sorting and stacking
- ◆ fine motor development

MATERIALS: book about Eskimos
sugar cubes
balloons
glue

ACTIVITY: Read about Eskimos to the children. Talk about how igloos were built and what materials were used. Discuss the Eskimos' way of life. Blow balloons into small circles. Children glue sugar cubes to the top half of the balloon (be sure they use glue on all sides of the sugar cubes). Let dry, then pop the balloons.

VARIATION: Count the sides of the cubes and the total number of cubes for a Math project. Enjoy an Eskimo Pie treat.

MATERIALS: windmill pattern
book about Netherlands/Holland
paper/ glue
tissue paper
pipe cleaners
fasteners
markers

PREPARATION: Use the windmill pattern to make copies of windmills.

ACTIVITY: Show children pictures of the traditional dress, landscape, windmills, buildings, and flowers of the Netherlands. Have the children cut out the windmills. Fasten the arms of the windmill so they turn. Using tissue paper, children can make tulips and other flowers to decorate around their windmills.

 Pre-cut windmills and have toddlers fasten the arms. Pre-cut small squares of tissue paper so the children can glue flowers onto the windmills.

School age children can make hats, wooden shoes, and other items from the Netherlands. Research and draw a Netherlands map with pictures showing products and points of interest.

CONCEPTS:
- ◆ Holland/Netherlands culture and windmills
- ◆ tradition
- ◆ mapping
- ◆ fine motor skills

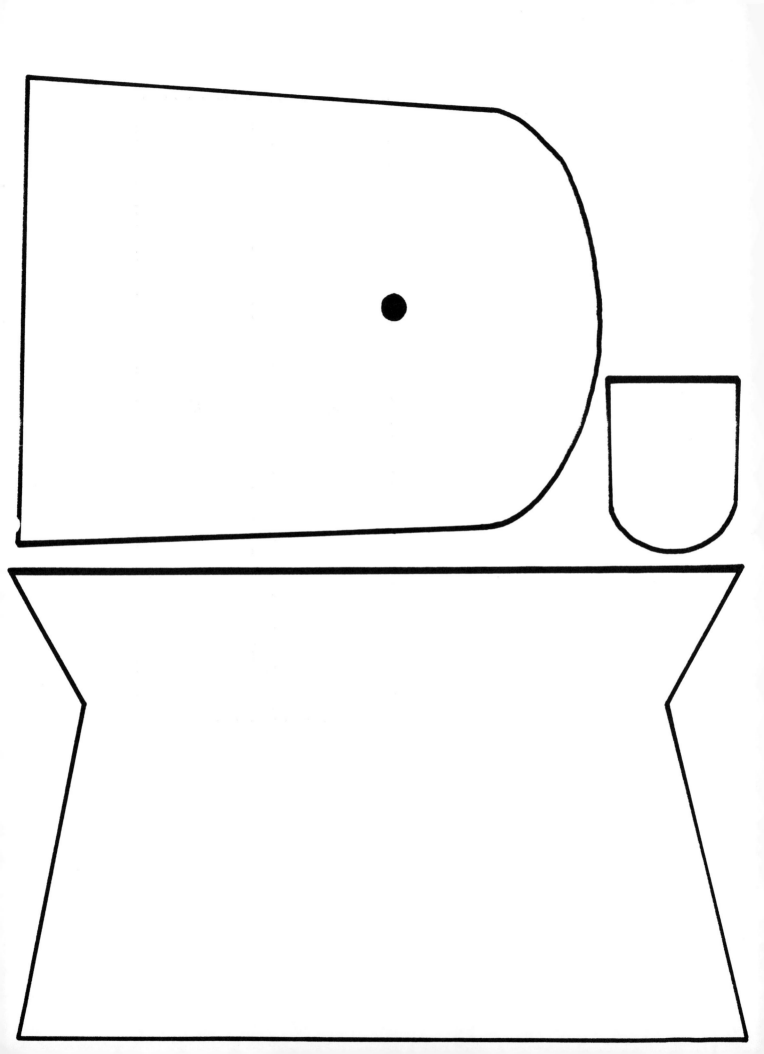

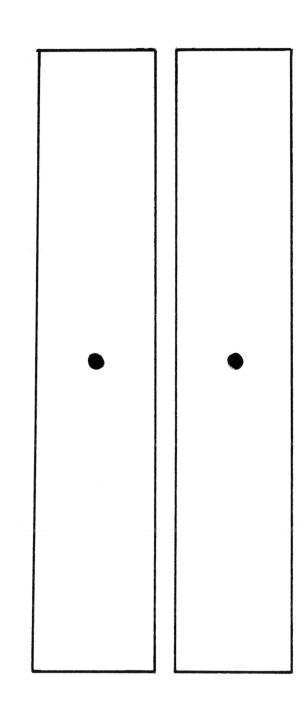

MATERIALS: book about Japan
paper
markers
stapler

ACTIVITY: Have a discussion about the Japanese culture using pictures as a visual aid. Talk about the traditional dress and how it is used today. With markers, children decorate a piece of paper in Japanese style. Fold the paper to resemble fans and staple at the bottom.

Older infants and toddlers can use crayons to color paper. Fold the fans for them. Show the children how a fan is used.

Using a Japanese cookbook, school age children can find an easy Japanese dish to prepare for the other children. Make name cards for the table and have children decorate them with Japanese letters.

CONCEPTS:
- Japanese culture
- folding
- Nutrition
- fine motor skills

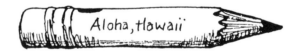

MATERIALS: book on Hawaii
box of tissues
crepe paper
yarn
scissors

ACTIVITY: Read about Hawaii. Show pictures of the islands, traditions, dress, foods, volcanoes, and other points of interest. After an open discussion about Hawaii, make flower leis using the tissues. Fold tissues back and forth as discussed in the previous Japanese fan activity. Tie yarn in the middle of the folded tissue. Carefully pull the two-ply tissue apart to form a pom pom. Make enough flowers to tie together to make a lei.

Make grass skirts by stapling strips of crepe paper to a premeasured piece of yarn. Keep stapling strips onto the yarn until there is enough crepe paper to cover the body and enough yarn left to tie the skirt around the waist.

 Older infants and toddlers will love wearing premade leis. Toddlers can participate in helping you make their grass skirts and in dancing.

 Have older children help preschoolers with their leis. Children can make up a hoola dance, creating their own hand movements to symbolize words. Have the children perform their dance and explain the meaning.

CONCEPTS:
- ◆ Hawaii and Hawaiian culture
- ◆ islands
- ◆ volcano
- ◆ fine motor skills
- ◆ dancing/movement

VARIATION: Together, prepare a Hawaiian luau for a follow up in Nutrition. Find a record or tape at your library or store and have the children listen and dance the hoola for a Music activity. Learn new Hawaiian words and their meanings for language development. Construct a volcano using clay (pour a mixture of baking soda, vinegar, and red food color inside the clay volcano for an "eruption" effect) and discuss volcanoes for a Science activity.

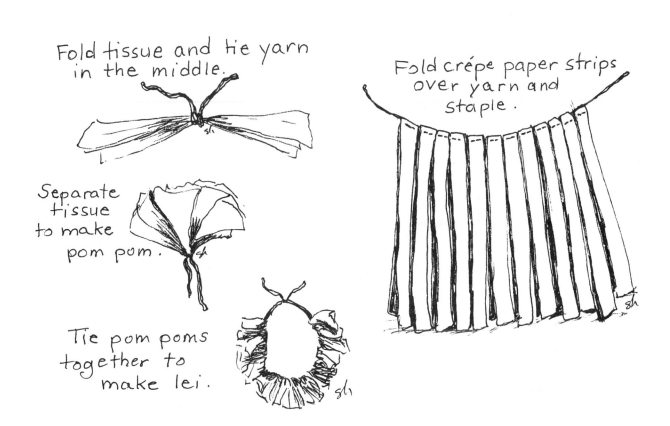

Fold tissue and tie yarn in the middle.

Separate tissue to make pom pom.

Tie pom poms together to make lei.

Fold crépe paper strips over yarn and staple.

MATERIALS: book about Australia
koala pattern
paper
scissors
glue

PREPARATION: Copy the koala pattern from Chapter 5 on brown or gray construction paper. Copy the tree branch pattern on a contrasting color.

ACTIVITY: Discuss the following categories of interest about Australia.

1. Animals	2. Games/Leisure	3. Famous For:	4. People	5. Nature
kangaroo	surfing	sugar cane	Aborigines	Great Barrier Reef
platypus	sailing	prospecting gold	British colon-	desert
dingo	"tree topping"	sheep/cattle	izers	farmland
wombat	"bowls"	farming		rainforests
koala				Eucalyptus trees
Tasmanian devil				

Be sure to use library books with an abundance of colorful pictures to keep younger children interested. Follow up the lesson with the children cutting koalas and gluing them to the tree branches.

ALL

Note: A wonderful reinforcement activity to this lesson would include the viewing of the animated movie "The Rescuers Down Under"; (it shows Australian animals, geographical settings, and culture).

CONCEPTS:
- ◆ Australia
- ◆ Australian culture and people
- ◆ group discussion
- ◆ vocabulary

ACTIVITY: Pick a famous river. Help the children find books and other information about that river.

Choose some of the following activities:

-Draw pictures or diagrams of the river.

-Write a story about a trip down the river.

-Write about and illustrate the animals that use the river as their habitat.

-Make a list of ways people use the river.

-Design and build (with popsicle sticks) a bridge or boat to cross the river.

CONCEPTS:

- ◆ geographical studies
- ◆ river habitats
- ◆ creative design and thinking
- ◆ language development

MATERIALS: Road Atlas
paper
pencils/markers
ruler

ACTIVITY: Have children look through an Atlas of the United States and find funny city names, unusual names of points of interest, and landmarks. Write a list of those places. Instruct the children to see how many rivers, mountain ranges, lakes, deserts, and forests they can find. Try graphing these natural landmarks to compare.

CONCEPTS:

- ◆ geographical skills
- ◆ map reading
- ◆ graphing
- ◆ problem-solving

MATERIALS: brochures from travel agency
paper
pencils
suitcase

ACTIVITY: Visit a local travel agency and ask for brochures about several different vacations. After returning home, show the children the different places to vacation.
Ask how many different types of transportation could get them to each place. Decide which vacation the group wants to take. Discuss what they want to see and do, how they will travel there, and where they will stay. Have the children draw imaginary tickets (airplane, train) to use

on their trip. Role-play the packing of a suitcase. Ask the children what they need to pack in the suitcase. Each time someone has an idea, let that child make believe he or she is putting that item into the suitcase. Set up an imaginary airplane, train, car, bus, or boat and act out going on vacation. Follow up the activity by arranging a field trip to a bus or train station or airport.

 Infants and toddlers may not be able to contribute to the discussion but involve them in the suitcase packing and role-playing (traveling, eating in restaurants, sightseeing).

 The children can make phone calls to inquire about prices for the vacation. Help them make a vacation budget to see what the imaginary trip will cost. They can also map out a route using a Road Atlas, figure travel time, and make sightseeing lists.

CONCEPTS:
- transportation
- geographical locations
- creative role-playing
- social development
- money comprehension
- problem-solving
- organizational skills

Chapter 7:

Creating is Elating-
Arts and Crafts

Chapter 7 Introduction

Until now, Arts and Crafts have been included in other activities as teaching tools. In this chapter, the purpose of Arts and Crafts projects is to enhance creativity and to have fun in the process. Objectives include developing fine motor skills, hand-eye coordination, expression, and creative thought. Many activities can be modified for various educational subjects. By using a wide range of materials, you can encourage and stimulate creativity. While both the children and you enjoy the process!

Painting is always a fun activity for children. The following section will show how painting can be even more exciting if you experiment with different techniques and materials. Painting reinforces fine motor skills and gives children a variety of options to help them develop creativity. Be sure to tape their paper to the work surface. See Chapter Two for teaching painting techniques.

ALL: All the children can have fun participating in these activities. Older infants will need assistance, a high chair, and protective covering.

CREAM PAINTING

ACTIVITY: Children spray whipped or shaving cream onto paper. Add drops of food coloring and let them paint with their fingers.

CORN SYRUP PAINTING

ACTIVITY: Using a brush or fingers, children dip into bowls of corn syrup and create! (See corn syrup recipe in Chapter two).

PUDDING PAINTING

ACTIVITY: Mix instant pudding and desired food colors. Children use fingers and hands. This is a delicious way to paint.

COOKIE PAINTING

ACTIVITY: Children paint on precooked sugar cookies using the egg yolk paint. (See egg yolk paint recipe in Chapter two).

STRAW BLOWN PAINTING

ACTIVITY: Spoon tempera paint onto paper and let children blow the paint with straws. See the magical designs appear before your eyes!

PIPE CLEANER PAINTING

ACTIVITY: Instead of brushes, the children can experiment with dipping pipe cleaners into paint to create lovely pictures.

TIE-DYE TISSUE PAINTING

ACTIVITY: Crumple tissue paper or crinkled paper and dip into the paint to create a unique effect.

CORRUGATED PAINTING

ACTIVITY: Brush paint onto corrugated paper. Press painted side onto a separate piece of paper to make prints.

TISSUES AND TOWELS

ACTIVITY: Paint on tissues or paper towels for a tie dye effect. For symmetrical designs, fold paper towel several times and dip corners into paint. Open the towels to see the surprise design.

CHALK IT UP

ACTIVITY: Using chalk, color a picture on paper. Paint over the pictures with watercolors.

SCRATCH PAINTS

ACTIVITY: With crayons, color designs on paper. Tempera paint over the crayon designs. After the paint dries, use a toothpick to scratch off paint to form pictures

SHORTENING PAINTING

ACTIVITY: Finger paint with shortening. Using watercolors, paint over the shortening for desired effects.

RUBBER CEMENT OR WAX PAINTING

Use rubber cement or drip wax onto paper to form a picture or design. Paint over the entire picture. Rubbing off the rubber cement or wax will leave a contrast and create a unique picture.

DISAPPEARING PAINT

ACTIVITY: Paint a picture using lemon or orange juice. Press with an iron to see the picture.

TEXTURE PAINTING

ACTIVITY: Place leaves, doilies, raised greeting cards, or other items with texture.

SPLATTER PICTURES

ACTIVITY: Gather up the smocks, paint, old toothbrushes and paper. Plan a little field trip to a vacant lot or woodsy area where creativity will not be stifled because of a mess. Dip toothbrushes into tempera paint and splatter the onto the paper. Splattering can be done by a flick of the wrist or using a spare finger to rub across the bristles. Be sure to point out colors that mix together to make other colors.

Technically, mosaics are pictures or designs that can be made by laying down tiles, colored stones, and other similar types of textile material. A collage is made with pieces of paper, textured materials, cloth, and other materials in part or entirely and is attached to a background. The activities found here could be classified as one or the other, or both, therefore they will all fall under one category. Subjects for magazine collages can be found in Chapter Two. Here is a sample mosaic/collage activity called Tropical Fish:

MATERIALS: suggested materials:
(popcorn, macaroni, colored spices, dry beans, craft tiles, tissue paper,etc.)
cardboard
glue

PREPARATION: With a black marker, draw a picture of a fish on each cardboard.

ACTIVITY: Children glue materials onto the cardboard fish and form patterns. The children can become more creative depending upon the amount of materials.

 The sizes of materials used in each activity will help to determine older infant and toddler participation. If a child can pick up the materials with assistance, they can place the materials onto the glue. Discuss the materials and finished products.

In each activity, school age children should be allowed more freedom to explore their creativity. Encourage them to design their own pictures and not utilize the patterns provided for the younger children.

CONCEPTS:
- ◆ pattern
- ◆ design
- ◆ creative thought
- ◆ fine motor skills

VARIATIONS: Using the same technique and a variety of materials, try experimenting with other mosaic/collage ideas.

1. Nursery rhymes: Draw pictures of favorite rhymes for the children to design.
2. Sugar cube designs: Paint sugar cubes in different colors. On cardboard, glue cubes into various designs.
3. Nut bowls: Make nut bowls using clay. While the clay is still soft, push materials into the clay to form designs.
4. Tissue paper: Cut 1" squares of different colored tissue paper. Dip middle of squares into glue and attach to a piece of paper. Using numerous squares, form designs or pictures. Predraw patterns for younger children to follow.
5. Tile mosaics: Older children will have fun using 1/2" or 1" construction tiles to design pictures onto cardboard.

MATERIALS: ink pads
paper
pens/markers
package craft eyes (optional)

ACTIVITY: Create animals, flowers, imaginary creatures and other pictures by pressing fingers or thumbs onto an ink pad and transferring prints to the paper. Use pens or markers to add and create features.

 Young children will thrill in just seeing their prints on the paper. Do not worry about recognizable designs or pictures.

Create cartoon characters and write captions or stories to accompany the prints.

CONCEPTS
- ◆ creative thinking
- ◆ fine motor development
- ◆ problem-solving

VARIATIONS: Use the fingerprints as Math counting tools for toddlers and preschool children. Each time the children add a new print, count all the prints on the paper. Write the number of prints at the top of the paper.

MATERIALS: paper plates/ pipe cleaners
construction paper (green/blue/yellow)
blue paint/brushes
fastener
glue/scissors

PREPARATION: Predraw a neck, head, yellow circles, and strips for feathers.

ACTIVITY: Children cut pieces for peacock and assemble them onto a large piece of paper. Glue all the pieces except the neck and head. Paint the paper plate and circles inside the yellow circles. Children add eyes and beaks by cutting shapes and glueing. Cut pipe cleaners into 3" strips to make feathers for the top of the head. Attach the head to the neck by gluing. Use a fastener to attach the base of the neck to the body. This will make the neck and head moveable.

 Display the peacock where infants can see. Tell the child all about peacocks. Describe and point to the peacocks.

 After precutting the peacock pieces for the toddlers, direct their gluing. Then they are ready to paint and decorate on their own.

CONCEPTS:
- ◆ fine motor skills
- ◆ following directions
- ◆ creative thought
- ◆ building
- ◆ problem-solving

VARIATION: Use this craft as a science project to study peacocks or as a follow-up about birds; visit the nearest zoo to conduct a closer study of birds.

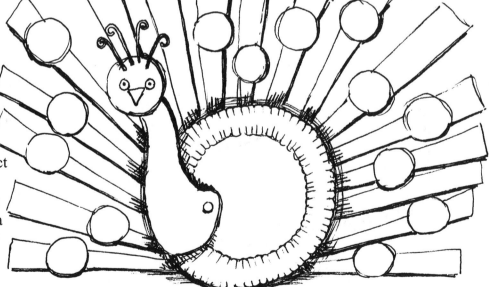

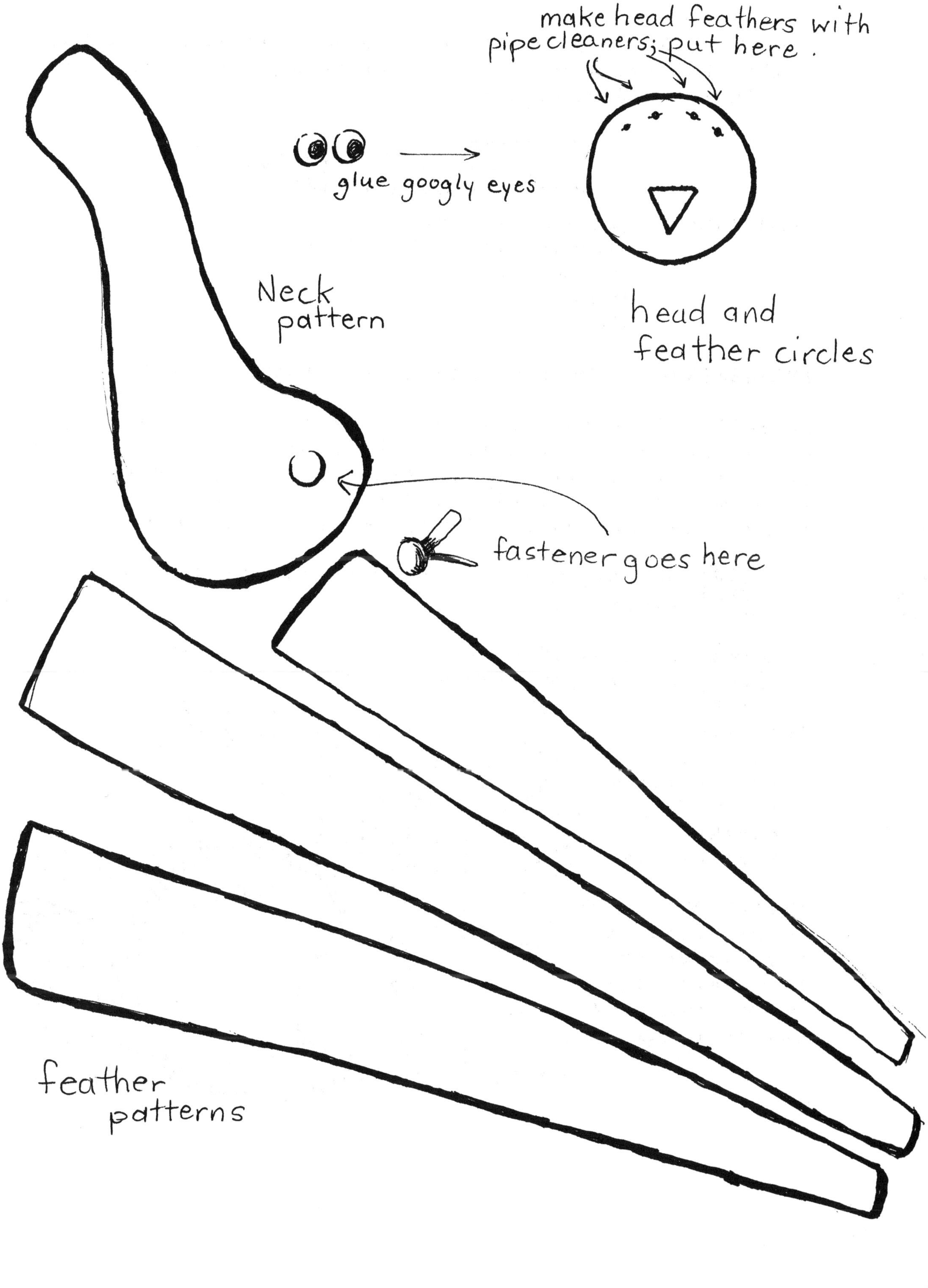

make head feathers with
pipe cleaners; put here.

glue googly eyes

head and
feather circles

Neck
pattern

fastener goes here

feather
patterns

MATERIALS: glue

glitter (all colors)

variety of materials: (pieces of wood, paper plates, paper, tissue paper, styrofoam meat trays, cups, etc.)

ACTIVITY: Children choose a material from the list. Allow them the freedom to decide the material, design, color, or themes. By drawing with the glue, children can create pictures or designs on their chosen material. Sprinkle with glitter.

Give children a cotton swab and a lid of glue. Paper is an easier material for young children. Help with gluing; sprinkle glitter for infants.

Children can be offered a subject or theme to recreate on their material.

CONCEPTS:
- ◆ fine motor skills
- ◆ creative thinking
- ◆ design and pattern
- ◆ texture
- ◆ color

VARIATION: Glittery Glue can be used in follow-up activities for Reading. Draw pictures to illustrate stories or poems. Practice writing letters or names using glitter. Holiday activities can be enhanced by using glitter art for cards, ornaments, and other decorations.

MATERIALS: newspaper print or large roll paper

pencils/markers

glue

scissors

miscellaneous materials: buttons, cloth, yarn, craft eyes, etc.

ACTIVITY: Tape a piece of paper (large enough for each child) to the floor. The children lay flat on the paper. Trace around each child to form a silhouette. Using a variety of materials, children can make hair, clothes, pockets, eyes, and other decorations on their silhouettes.

CONCEPTS:
- ◆ creative thought
- ◆ self-awareness

♦ problem-solving

VARIATIONS: Try using silhouettes of hands
and feet to create unique designs or pictures. Try
some of these ideas: compare sizes and make comparison charts as a Math activity for preschoolers
and school age children. Animal pictures can be
used to reinforce Science lessons.

MATERIALS: broken crayons
                    construction paper
                    iron/board
                    cheese grater
                    newspapers
                    waxed paper
                    scissors

PREPARATION: Older children can <u>carefully</u> grate broken crayons into shavings. Fold
construction paper in half and cut a square from the folded side to form a frame. Precut sheets of
waxed paper large enough to cover the hole inside the frame.

ACTIVITY: Sprinkle multicolored crayon shavings into a design on the waxed paper. Cover
the design with another piece of waxed paper. Set several layers of newspaper onto the ironing
board and place the waxed paper designs on the newspaper. Cover the waxed paper designs with
a few more pages of newspaper. With a hot iron, <u>assist the children in carefully</u> ironing over the
newspaper. The crayons will melt into a beautiful design. Tape the waxed paper designs to the
frame and hold them up to the light. When completed, the children will want to hang them in the
window for a stained glass effect.

 Although infants are too young to participate in the creation of the stained glass,
they will surely enjoy looking through the light at them with you. Hang one in
their bedroom window so they can watch the light filter through the colors.

 Placing the crayon shavings on the waxed paper is a task the toddler can easily
master. <u>The ironing should be left to the adults or older children.</u> Show the
children how to attach the waxed paper to the frames.

 Cut larger pieces of waxed paper. With a toothpick, children draw pictures onto
the waxed paper. Using separate colors, fill in the picture with crayon shaving. As
a follow up, research the history of stained glass and share the information with
the rest of the children.

CONCEPTS:
- ◆ design
- ◆ creative thought
- ◆ fine motor skills
- ◆ problem-solving

MATERIALS: scarf or material for blindfold
paper
crayons

ACTIVITY: Choose any simple object or item for the children to draw. A person, animal, type of scenery, household item, or type of transportation are a few examples. After the children are sitting at a table, blindfold each child. Give directions step by step on how to draw the item you have chosen (person: draw a head, attach a skinny body, add arms and legs, make a silly face). When the drawings are finished, remove the blindfolds so the children can see what they have done. It is fun to see how close they are to completing the item or how funny their drawings have become.

 Older children can have turns giving directions. Suggest using descriptive or action words to increase vocabulary and stimulate ideas.

CONCEPTS:
- ◆ listening skills
- ◆ coordination
- ◆ memory
- ◆ creative thinking
- ◆ problem-solving

MATERIALS: construction paper (two or more colors)
glue

ACTIVITY: Choose a shape from any holiday or subject. Tear the paper into that shape and glue onto a contrasting colored piece of paper.

 Infants can tear paper into pieces. Glue their torn shapes onto another piece of paper.

 Toddlers can tear pieces of paper. Allow them the freedom to glue pieces without forming any concrete idea.

To challenge older children, have them rip whole pictures into shapes and creating an entire scene.

CONCEPTS:
- ◆ hand-eye coordination
- ◆ creative development
- ◆ fine motor skills

MATERIALS: paper
markers

PREPARATION: Write a list of silly names of nonexistent creatures. Here are a few to get started:

1. giraffamonk	4. zappabird
2. kinkablub	5. weasalink
3. baboonoroo	6. octophant

ACTIVITY: Tell the children they are taking a trip to a zoo from another world. Give them the names of some of the creatures in the zoo and have them use their imaginations to draw these creatures. When their pictures are completed, ask questions, such as: "Where do the creatures live?" "What do they eat?" and "How do they behave?"

 School age children can write their own lists of silly creatures. Choose one from the list and write a story about that creature. Draw a picture of the zoo with many of the creatures. Encourage further creativity by asking the children to design a zoo that is unlike any they have ever seen.

CONCEPTS:
- ◆ stimulate imagination
- ◆ develop creative thought
- ◆ problem-solving
- ◆ language art skills

MATERIALS: posterboard
yarn, string or laces
construction paper
marker/paper punch

ACTIVITY: Using markers and construction paper, design a picture (or cut and glue pictures from magazines). Paper punch holes around the pictures. The children use the pictures as sewing cards by lacing yarn, string or laces through the holes.

 Punch holes into the toddler's pictures. Hold the sewing card while showing the toddler where to place the end of the yarn. Pull the yarn through and keep assisting until the toddler can accomplish the task alone or until it becomes tedious.

 Instead of designing pictures onto paper, the school age child can draw his or her designs onto wood. Allow them to hammer nails along the outline of their designs. Tie yarn or string onto one nail. Take the yarn or string to each nail, wrap it around once and go to another nail until the outline is complete. Use additional pieces of yarn or string in the same manner to create designs inside the outline.

CONCEPTS:
- hand-eye coordination
- fine motor skills
- design/patterns
- creative thought

Face Painting

MATERIALS: colored face chalk, paint, or crayons (be sure product is specifically made
        for using on children's faces)
    make-up, eyeliner pencil, and brushes
    baby powder and large (2" wide soft bristles) make-up brush
    safe, free standing mirror

ACTIVITY: With the children, brainstorm ideas for pictures to paint. Children may be interested in looking like a particular favorite character or maybe they would like individual pictures. Children can decide if they want to create designs on their own faces or possibly someone else's face. Older children can paint infants' and toddlers' faces. When the painting is completed, put baby powder into a bowl and dip the large make-up brush into the powder. Dab the powder lightly over all the painted areas and blow off excess powder (be sure the children hold their breath, so the powder is not inhaled). This will help keep the make-up from smearing. Below are a few pattern ideas to get you started, in case the children would like you to paint something on their faces.

ALL

CONCEPTS:
- creative thought
- group discussion

◆ fine motor skills

VARIATION: Read a storybook aloud to the children for a Reading activity. Children can try painting their faces to look like different characters from the book. If studies for the day include letter recognition, follow-up with writing the letters on faces!

MATERIALS: yarn or string
crayons
paper

ACTIVITY: Instruct the children to place yarn or string on a table. Encourage them to move the yarn to form designs or pictures. Using several pieces of different sized yarn or string is also an option. When the design is in a desired formation on the table, place a piece of paper on top. Rub bare crayons across the paper and the design underneath will appear.

ALL

CONCEPTS:
- creative thinking
- design
- fine motor skills

MATERIALS: white posterboard
crayons
black paint/brushes
paper clips

PREPARATION: Cut posterboard into smaller pieces.

ACTIVITY: Using a variety of light colored crayons, children color their entire piece of posterboard. With the black paint, paint over the colored area. Let dry. Open the paper clips and scratch on the black paint to draw pictures.

 Here is a chance for the younger children to scribble with crayons. Direct painting. Let them scratch the black paint by using a less sharp utensil (ie: the end of a spoon).

 Encourage older children to make detailed etchings, intricate designs, or pictures using a theme.

CONCEPTS:
- following directions
- design
- creative thought

- ◆ sequence
- ◆ problem-solving

MATERIALS: toilet paper rolls
string
tape
glue

ACTIVITY: Using glue, children connect the two paper rolls side by side to resemble binoculars. After the rolls have dried, poke holes at the top of the outside of each roll. They can tie an end of the string through each hole so the binoculars can be worn around the neck. If desirable, crayons, markers, paint or stickers can be used to decorate the binoculars.

ALL

CONCEPTS:
- ◆ hand-eye coordination
- ◆ fine motor skills
- ◆ creative thought
- ◆ stringing

VARIATIONS: Use the binoculars in a Science unit for birdwatching. Go on a nature hike and draw pictures of all the different birds that are seen through the "binoculars". Write stories about the birds or make the book "Birds I Saw on Our Hike" for Reading. Save a box full of toilet paper rolls. Give the children an opportunity to play, build, and create anything they wish by using the rolls.

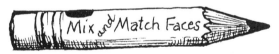

MATERIALS: light cardboard/face pattern
construction paper
scissors
markers

PREPARATION: Draw a face pattern onto the light cardboard with a black marker; a simple oval is fine.

ACTIVITY: Children cut the faces out of the cardboard. Direct children to draw eyes, mouth, nose, hair, and eyebrows in appropriate sections of the face. With additional paper, children can cut ears, hats, bows, mustaches, and other enhancements. When each face is completed, cut along the dotted lines. Get the children together to mix and match faces. See how many silly people they can create.

 Toddlers will love to use the created faces as puzzles. Instead of drawing their own face parts, cut parts for them to glue.

Have the children create names and stories for each character they invent.

CONCEPTS:
- ◆ creative thinking
- ◆ facial discrimination
- ◆ problem-solving
- ◆ fine motor skills
- ◆ color

VARIATIONS: Use the face patterns for the following themes: Circus (clowns), Careers (different types of workers), Famous People (historical figures), Small World (children around the world), Family and Friends (self-portraits, family and friends), etc.

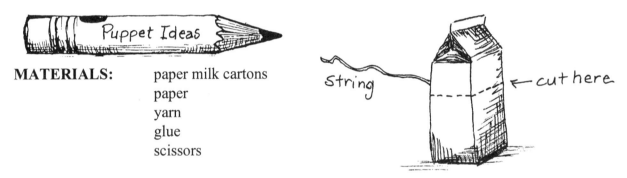

MATERIALS: paper milk cartons
paper
yarn
glue
scissors

PREPARATION: Cover the milk cartons with paper. Using a razor knife, cut the front and sides of the carton as shown in the diagram. On colored paper, draw circles for eyes, nose, muzzle, and spots. Oval shapes can be drawn for ears and tail.

ACTIVITY: Children cut out the circles and glue them onto the carton to form their pooches. Glue ears to the upper sides making sure the glue does not extend past the slit in the carton. Poke a small hole in the upper back section so children can string their yarn. Tie a knot inside and outside the carton so the yarn stays in place. The puppet talks by pulling the yarn.

 Precut and direct the children's gluing. Show the little ones how to make the puppies talk. Encourage play-acting.

 Give the children plenty of paper and craft materials to make other types of animals or to invent new creatures. Older children can read a story to the younger ones by using the puppets as visual aids.

CONCEPTS:

- ◆ reinforce cutting skills
- ◆ creative thought
- ◆ role-playing
- ◆ language development

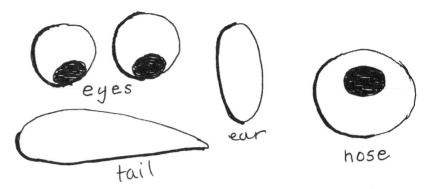

VARIATIONS: Build a stage and have children use their imaginations to perform skits and plays with their puppets. Other puppets can be created by using paper sacks, cloth or felt, sticks with cut pictures, old socks, or papier-mache' heads with cloth bodies. Use the puppets to reinforce literature or your current theme (story characters, animals, people).

MATERIALS: plastic gallon milk jugs
pink and other paint colors
paper
scissors
glue

PREPARATION: Cut slots in the top of the milk jugs. Prepare the painting area with newspapers.

ACTIVITY: Have each child paint her entire jug with pink paint. When dried, use different colors to decorate the pigs with eyes, nostrils, flowers, hearts and various designs. Curly tails can be cut from construction paper and glued to the back end of the pigs. Money can be removed by unscrewing the jug cap.

 Let infants play with the unpainted plastic jugs. Buy decorative stickers for them to Put on their pigs. Older infants may be able to paint with guidance.

 Toddlers will do well with the painting. Some assistance may be needed. Count for the children while they put their pennies into the finished bank. Children must be supervised with coins.

 After the banks are completed, give the children a variety of coins. Have them practice money values by counting the coins as they put them into their banks.

CONCEPTS:

- ◆ hand-eye coordination
- ◆ design
- ◆ monetary values
- ◆ creative thought

◆ form/color

VARIATION: Follow up the craft with a Math lesson in coin value and counting. Visit a bank and discover how the system of banking works. For a Science activity, conduct a study about pigs. Visit a farm and watch the lifestyle and activity. To reinforce Nutrition concepts, search in magazines for pictures of food made from pork. Read stories with pig characters or write pig stories for Reading and Language.

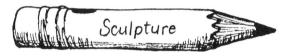

Typically, when people think of "sculpture," they think of famous works created by people like Michelangelo. Along with painting, sculpture is one of the oldest art forms in history. Clay, stone and metal structures instantly pop into mind. However, sculpting can be accomplished by using any desired materials along with the imagination. The following activities show different materials, ideas, and age recommendations you can try with your children.

FOIL SCULPTING
Use foil to form animals, people, and objects. All children can participate.

PIPE CLEANERS
Pipe cleaners can be bent, connected, twisted, and formed into all kinds of creations. Under close supervision, all children can participate.

PLAYDOUGH/CLAY
These are all-time favorites. Play dough is easier to mold and form than clay. Toothpicks are a fun addition to the building process. Give the children ideas or themes to practice, then allow them the freedom to experiment and create. Clay is recommended for the older children. **Neither play dough nor clay is recommended for infants.**

PAPER SCULPTING
The local library should have books about paper folding, origami, and paper airplanes. Preschoolers can handle very simple folding directions. Older children love the challenge of difficult patterns. Using the paper sculptures, make mobiles for infants and toddlers to hang.

ICE CREAM STICKS
With a little glue and a lot of ice creams sticks, the children will be able to design buildings, spaceships, animals, or even abstract objects. Encourage complete freedom and imagination. **Sticks are not recommended for infants, and toddlers need supervision.**

STUFFED KITES
Cut two pieces of paper into identical desired kite shapes. Tape the edges together but leave an opening. Stuff the kite with paper towels for a dimensional effect. Infants and toddlers will enjoy crumpling the paper towels and stuffing the kites. Older children will want to see how unique they can make their kite designs.

PIÑATAS

Piñatas are great fun for kids, and easy, too. Let the children decide on a subject for the piñata (fish, bear, unicorn, etc.). Blow up a balloon and cover it with papier-mache. Be sure to leave a small spot open to put candy in later. Build up necessary areas with newspaper and paste to form the chosen subject. Have the children work together on one piñata. After the balloon is dry, the children glue on colored, two-inch square tissue paper until the papier-mache' is covered. Infants and toddlers can help stick tissue paper onto the object. Have preschool and older children cut additional decorations (eyes, ears, horns, etc.) from construction paper and glue onto the sculpture. Let the smaller children participate in filling the piñata with goodies. Everyone can join in the fun when it is time for the blindfold and breaking of the piñata.

SOAP CARVING

Using soap for sculpting is an exciting way to create. Draw outline of desired object with a sculpting knife and then shave the unwanted soap away. This requires a sharper tool, so the activity should be restricted to older school age children.

MOBILES AND STABILES

Mobiles can be made by hanging created objects on string, yarn or wire. Set out a variety of materials and just let the children design anything that comes to mind. A stabile is built from a stable source (such as wood or a chunk of clay). Wire can be attached to a base and objects can be designed on the end of each wire. This activity is recommended for preschool through school age children, however, infants and toddlers will enjoy the finished products and may even be able to assist in connecting the items.

CONCEPTS:
- ◆ development of imagination and creativity
- ◆ problem-solving
- ◆ design
- ◆ sculpting
- ◆ dimensions
- ◆ fine motor development
- ◆ exposure to variety of materials
- ◆ form/texture

VARIATIONS: These sculpting ideas can also be used in other subjects to reinforce concepts. Read a story and use an activity to make a character or scene from that story. For Math, build numbers or items to use in the computation of math facts or as hands-on manipulatives. When studying flowers, animals, planets, or other Science themes, follow up the activity with a sculpture that coincides. Build food items to reinforce Nutrition concepts. Use sculpting to design new buildings, to create families, or to re-create cultures to enhance your Social Studies curriculum.

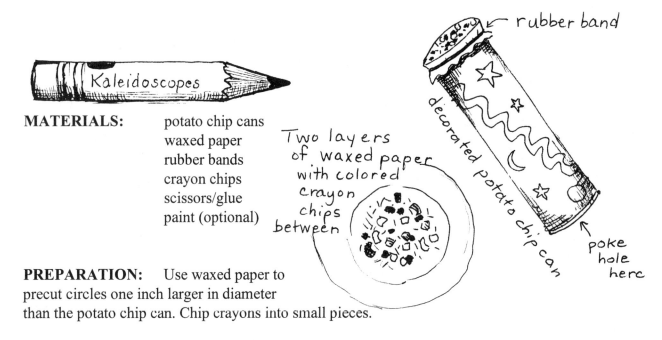

Kaleidoscopes

MATERIALS: potato chip cans
waxed paper
rubber bands
crayon chips
scissors/glue
paint (optional)

PREPARATION: Use waxed paper to precut circles one inch larger in diameter than the potato chip can. Chip crayons into small pieces.

ACTIVITY: Paint the outside of the cans if desirable to you and the children. After the cans are dried, the children can sprinkle different colored chips of crayons onto one waxed paper circle. Glue around the outside of the circle and place another circle of waxed paper over the chips. Cover one open side of the can with the dried waxed paper circles and attach with a rubber band. To view, poke a hole in the opposite side of the can and slowly turn the can.

 If you are daring, let older infants use finger paints to decorate cans. Infants can play with potato chip cans. Use extra cans for infants to practice filling and emptying objects. Show them how to look through the hole at the pretty colors.

 Toddlers can join in the fun, too, but will require your help when placing the rubber band over the waxed paper circles. Use extra cans for sorting objects.

 After finishing the activity, have the children research the history of kaleidoscopes.
Design a new and improved kaleidoscope.

CONCEPTS:
- fine motor skills
- color
- design
- problem-solving

Homemade Blooming

MATERIALS: construction paper
green pipe cleaners
tissue paper
glue/scissors

PREPARATION: Using a ruler and yellow construction paper, draw lines to cut and fold. Draw a petal pattern onto matching colored paper.

ACTIVITY: Follow the cut and fold lines where indicated on the paper. Cut out the petals. Curve the rectangle into a cylinder shape and glue or staple. Glue large fold down on center of leafy area. Attach the green pipecleaner to the back of the flower.

PREPARATION: Cut five or six 4" x 4" squares of tissue paper (any color or combination of colors).

ACTIVITY: Line up all the squares into one pile. Have the child place a finger into the center of the pile and grab the tissue paper from behind with the other hand. Fasten with string or staple. Make leaf backings using one green square and fasten with a green pipecleaner on the handle area.

PREPARATION: Cut 1 inch squares of blue tissue paper.

ACTIVITY: Twist each square in the middle. Attach the bluebells by twisting them around the pipe cleaner. If the bluebells do not stay fastened, glue or staple them to the pipe cleaner. Continue with as many squares as desired.

CONCEPTS:
- ◆ creative thought
- ◆ fine motor skills
- ◆ flower names and parts
- ◆ following directions

VARIATION: Decorate potato chip cans for vases. As an alternative to 3-dimensional flowers, glue tissue paper onto paper plate backgrounds to form sculptures.

DAFFODILS

yellow construction paper

| = cut line

----- = fold line

fold under and glue

pipe cleaner

ROSES

4"

4"

push

squeeze

fasten   pull out petals

BLUEBELLS

cut

twist

twist around pipe cleaner

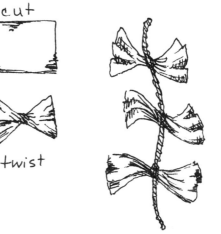

Chapter 8:

Magical Outlets-
Music and Dramatics

Chapter 8 Introduction

Creative outlets can be essential to a person's well-being and positive self-image. Children are very uninhibited and anxious to try new and exciting ways to create and express themselves. Music and Drama are two very useful ways to tap into a child's creativity. Music and Drama are also fun learning tools for a teacher or parent to use when integrating an entire learning curriculum. Children can develop skills and concepts in language, memory, listening, comprehension, self-expression, self-awareness, and more. Records, tapes, and CDs with songs that reinforce letters, number, counting, and color recognition can be purchased to further enhance your program.

All great homemade puppets (and store bought ones) need a place to perform. Let's make a stage and watch the characters come alive!

MATERIALS: large rectangular box
paints/brushes
colorful crepe paper
glue/scissors
razor knife
2 yards of fabric
skinny pole or curtain rod
hot glue

PREPARATION: Cut the lids from the box top. Cut a rectangle from the bottom of the box for the performers' arms and another rectangle from the side of the box for an opening to the stage. Next, take the fabric and fold the material over about 2" and sew a pocket for the curtain rod. Hem the bottom of the curtain.

ACTIVITY: This is a very open-ended project. Creativity and flexibility are the keys. Allow children to design pictures to glue to the stage. Paint decorations or use crepe paper for different effects. Separate pieces of rectangular cardboard can be decorated for backdrop scenery. When the stage is dry, an **adult** can hot glue the ends of the curtain rods to the inside of the stage. Now the "stage is set" to create and perform puppet shows. Integrate music into the plays and performances.

VARIATIONS: Create shows to reinforce historical events and holiday themes.

CONCEPTS:
- creative thinking
- problem-solving
- color and design
- play acting

There are many wonderful children's musical soundtracks on the market today. Soundtracks from "The Sound of Music", "Mary Poppins", "Little Mermaid", "Aladdin", "Beauty and the Beast", and "Cinderella" are just a few. The children can spend time listening and singing along with the songs from these special movies, but there are other ways to utilize this music. Have the children choose a song, dress-up, make accessories and act out scenes from the movie. School age children also love to choreograph dance routines to the music and have performances for everyone. Using a tape player, the children can make up dance steps for each line in the song. After practicing those dance steps over and over, go onto the next line of the song until the dance routine is completed. Encourage children to use props with their routines (ie. jump ropes, beach balls, batons, hoola hoops).

Make believe is so much fun, especially when the topic is the circus! Gather the children together and have them name different acts and characteristics of the circus. Make a list of their ideas. Ask questions to help them formulate ideas about how to re-enact items from the list. Here are a few suggestions to get you started:

By using their imaginations, a few household props, some face paint and dress up materials, the children can recreate the whole circus environment.

ringmaster	tumbling act	clowns
elephant act	tightrope act	jugglers
lion tamer	concession person	ticket taker
dancers	balancing act	seal acts
dog show	clown acts	trapeze artists

This list of tapes and/or records can get you started in integrating music into your program. Buy or borrow a few tapes or records. Choose two or three songs to teach the children. After several weeks, begin adding a new song every day. Children love songs that require action along with singing (such as 'Skip to My Lou'). Make up finger actions to go along with songs (example: two fingers moving up and down for the rabbit in "Little Bunny Foo-Foo"). The more the children are using their bodies, the easier it will be for them to remember the songs. Allow the children to listen to the music. Sing the songs for them, and then have them join in. Repetition on a daily basis will help them remember the words and melodies. Children do participate more when you sing along with them.

<u>**REFERENCES FOR MUSIC**</u>

1. Fred Penner: <u>Happy Feet</u>, Oak Street Music/Dino Music, 1992.

2. Raffi:
- <u>Baby Beluga</u>, Troubadour Records.
- <u>In Concert with the Rise and Shine Band</u>, Troubadour Records, 1985.
- <u>One Light, One Sun</u>, Troubadour Records, 1985.
- <u>Singable Songs for the Very Young</u>, Troubadour Records, 1976.
- <u>Corner Grocery Store and Other Singable Songs</u>, Troubadour Records, 1979.

3. <u>Transitions 1</u>: Placenta Music, Inc., 1988. Soothing music for crying infants-lulls children to sleep.
   <u>Transitions 2</u>: Placenta Music, Inc., 1990. Soothing music for crying infants-lulls children to sleep.

4. Northstar Entertainment, Inc.: <u>Games for Rainy Days</u>; Northstar Entertainment, Inc., Atlanta, Georgia. Music and skill games for children and families.

5. Songwriters and Artists for the Earth (SAFE): <u>Put on Your Green Shoes</u>; Sony Music Entertainment, 1993. Science environmental music.

6. Classics for Kids: <u>Adventures of America</u>; Fun music.

7. The Jinglehimers: <u>Children's Favorites</u>; RCA, 1985. HRB Music Co., Inc., 1977, 1985. Fun, singalong music.

8. Sharon, Louis and Bram: <u>Mainly Mother Goose</u>; Elephant Records, Toronto, Canada. Includes movement, songs, math concepts and nursery rhymes.

If you have ever watched children who are listening to music, you know that the first thing to happen is their little bodies start wiggling. Movement seems to be a natural reaction to music in young and old alike. Movement is a way children can express what they are feeling in relationship to what they hear, and also begin to learn rhythm, beats, and patterns. Encourage some of the following "movement" exercises:

146

Extemporaneous Dance

Play music and let the children move in any way that feels good to them. Have them choose songs or favorite records.

Marching

Find tapes or records that have marching music. Line up the children and give them percussion type instruments or household items to bang to the beat of the music. Give them a demonstration of marching techniques (lifting their feet up high, moving their arms, standing straight). The children can dress up and have a little parade down your street (carry the tape cassette player along as they march).

Clapping Games

Make up games to include clapping activity. Play the "name" game where the children clap a certain number of times (say three), then they name someone they know, then they clap again and keep repeating the process. Keep a beat going so the game develops a pattern or rhythm. The patterns and words can become as complex as the age group allows.

Aerobics

Find a low impact aerobics tape that would be fun for you and the children. Richard Simmons' "Sweatin' to the Oldies" videos are very fun for children, as well as adults. Set aside a time during the week to spend 15 minutes exercising to the music. Not only is this a very healthy way to spend time, but it also gives the children a sense of beat, repetition, and rhythm.

Simon Says

Play a game of Simon Says to music. Have the music in the background while a leader tells the children to make certain movements. Encourage the movements to coincide with the music.

Musical Feet

Cut out little footprints from construction paper and spread around the floor. Play some background music and have the children move from one footprint to another in step with the music. If the music is slower, the transfer from one footprint to the other is slower.

Lip Sync

This is not really a typical movement activity but in reality the lips are moving to the music. Children love to "mouth" songs and this gives them an opportunity to connect with the words and rhythm of the music without worrying about the tones and notes. Organize a lip sync show so the children can perform their favorite songs.

CONCEPTS:
- rhythm
- pattern
- listening
- large motor development
- auditory perception

Make a list of easy songs children love to sing. Here are a few suggestions:

"I've Been Working on the Railroad"   "Oh! Suzanna"
"Kookaburra"   "Yankee Doodle"
"Twinkle, Twinkle, Little Star"   "London Bridge"

Gather the children in a group. Together, sing one of the songs from the list. Then tell the children that they are going to make up a new "silly" song by changing the word in each line and trying to rhyme the next line with that word. For example, the children may decide upon a tune like this:

"Twinkle, twinkle, little kite,
How I wonder what you bite.
Up above the sky so fun,
Like a diamond in a bun".

Whatever song they decide to change and re-rhyme, there will be much laughter and creative thinking!

CONCEPTS:
- problem-solving
- lyrics
- rhythm
- rhyme
- creative thinking

MATERIALS:

hats	blouses	vests	shirts	purses
belts	pants	skirts	dresses	ties
shoes	scarves	* any old items or costumes		

ACTIVITY: Purchase or make a wooden or plastic toy box for dress up attire. Keep the dress up container next to the housekeeping area. This is an open-ended activity and can be used during creative playing or as the wardrobe for role-playing activities and performing.

CONCEPTS:
- creative thought
- coordination
- language development
- vocabulary building

PREPARATION: Make a list of different action activities that can be acted out by the children (riding a bus, playing Frisbee, fishing, jumping rope, driving a car).

ACTIVITY: Have two children be partners. Tell the children that you want them to "make believe" they are actually doing one of the activities from the list. Encourage verbal and physical interaction, but try acting without the use of props.

 Children can show very simplified actions, such as talking on the telephone, throwing a ball, picking flowers, etc. Keep their participation to a "one on one" basis.

 Older children can help make up the list of actions for the younger children, or they can create more complex actions to act out with a partner. Using common tunes ("Old MacDonald" "Row Your Boat"), make up songs to go with each job title. Have a show for the younger children.

CONCEPTS:
- cooperation
- creative thought
- problem-solving
- hand/eye/body coordination
- communication skills (nonverbal)
- role-playing

VARIATION: Children can think of jobs they would like to do or what they want to be when they become adults. Each child can act out his or her ideal future role.

PREPARATION: Use the following list (or create your own ideas) of actions to write on small pieces of paper:

1. Smell something burning on the stove.
2. Eat a piece of pizza.
3. Hang a picture on the wall.
4. Ride your bike through a mud puddle.
5. Make an ice cream cone and eat it.
6. Mow and water the lawn.
7. Act like a particular animal involved in a particular action.
8. Take a roller coaster ride with a "pretend" friend.
9. Paint a particular scene on a canvas.

ACTIVITY: Each child selects a piece of paper and acts out that particular activity to the group. The group has to guess the action and figure out the details involved in the charade. The person who guesses correctly gets to be the next actor/actress.

Piggy-back songs are familiar tunes that have different lyrics. "Mary Had a Little Lamb", "London Bridge" and "Row, Row, Row Your Boat" are common tunes where the words have been changed to fit an objective or theme. These types of songs are very popular with young children. You can find numerous piggy-back songs in early childhood resource books. It is also just as easy and fun to create your own to fit your personal needs.

The first step is to choose any popular tune the children may recognize. Write down objectives from themes you are teaching. Then make up rhyming sentences to fit the tune and the rhythm. Here is one example created for a kindergarten class that was studying the Rain Forest in South America:

Down by the Amazon
(sung to: "Down by the Riverside")

Watch that monkey swinging by...
Down by the Amazon, down by the Amazon.
Down by the Amazon.
Watch that money swinging by...
Down by the Amazon,
Down by the Am-a-zon!

Watch that parrot flying by...
Up above the Amazon, up above the Amazon.
Up above the Amazon.
Watch that parrot flying by...
Up above the Amazon,
Up above the Am-a-zon!

Watch that jaguar creeping by...
Down by the Amazon, down by the Amazon...
Down by the Amazon.
Watch that jaguar creeping by...
Down by the Amazon,
Down by the Am-a-zon!

Note: Have the children think of verses after they have studied all the animals of the rainforest. Here are a few more suggested verses:

Watch the anaconda slither by..
Down in the Amazon, down in the Amazon...

Watch that boa squeezing by..
Down by the Amazon, down by the Amazon...

Watch those piranha swimming by...
Down in the Amazon, down in the Amazon...

MATERIALS: tea set
play dishes
juice/snacks
table cloth/napkins
tape player/tapes

ACTIVITY: Have a tea party each day with a new host or hostess. The hosts and hostesses can decide how to dress up and what to serve. Develop other ideas such as: invitations, food, favorite music to play, table settings, and decorations. While play acting, encourage children to develop creative thinking skills, social awareness, and manners.

MATERIALS: paper plates
magazines
glue/scissors
play money
construction paper
dress-up clothing

ACTIVITY: Children look through magazines to find pictures of food. Cut and glue meals onto paper plates. Decide on prices and names of dishes. Design a menu cover and menu. Once all the props are in order, take turns playing particular roles (waiter, hostess, customers, cashiers and so on). Use pads of paper to write down orders. Pass out money to customers so they know how much to spend and what they can afford to order. Have cashiers give change to reinforce mathematical concepts. Encourage children to decide what role they play (housewife, child, teacher, millionaire). Discuss the event after each role-playing episode. Set the atmosphere and include different kinds of music. If possible, find a variety of music (classical, country, Asian, Italian, jazz, rock) and let the children decide upon the type of music that should be played in each type of restaurant.

Infants and toddlers can easily play roles as themselves at the restaurant. Get high chairs and bibs. Have older children interact with them as they play their parts.

The bulk of the preparation of this activity can be handled by this age group. Encourage research to discover cultural differences.

CONCEPTS:
- ◆ problem-solving
- ◆ types of music

- food groups
- role-playing
- creative thinking
- monetary values
- careers
- cultural awareness

VARIATION: Instead of using a restaurant theme, try re-creating a dance hall establishment. Types of decorations, clothing, music and dances can be incorporated. The children can run the establishment, be patrons, or both.

Teach children to recognize different sounds in the music. Point out different instruments (that's a drum, piano, flute, etc.). See if they can clap when they hear each instrument. Find pictures of different instruments and glue onto cards. Give each child an instrument card. As they listen to different songs, they can hold up the instrument that they hear at different points in the song. If possible, demonstrate actual instruments to the children, so they can hear and associate the sounds with the visual appearance of each instrument.

 Have older children research the history of each instrument. Write reports and draw illustrations to go along with the information. Read the reports to the other children. Some older children may even play an instrument and enjoy demonstrating or giving a little concert for the younger children.

MATERIALS: large sheets of newsprint or paper
markers

^	= **stamp feet**
O	= **"oooh" sound**
	= **smack lips**
*	= **click fingers**
X	= **clapping**

PREPARATION: Draw a simple chart of different sound patterns enclosed in rectangles (see sample).

X X X X	**O O X ^**	**^ ^ * ☺**
⸮ ^ ☺ ^	**X X O ***	*** * * ☺**

Together with the children, perform this simple, unique composition. If you notice, the example has four beats to a measure. Be sure to have the right number of beats in each measure. Include rest marks, intonation marks, and other musical symbols that you want to introduce. Once the children havehad a taste of "composing", have them make up their own sound songs. When "composing" and performing become easier, then the children are ready to get into groups and make harmony. Each group (using the same number of beats in a measure for both groups) will compose their own sound songs then come together to perform the songs at the same time. Several groups can be formed to make more intricate masterpieces.

CONCEPTS:
- ◆ composition
- ◆ harmony
- ◆ measures
- ◆ beat/rhythm
- ◆ creative thought
- ◆ problem-solving

VARIATION: A variety of rhythm instruments can be substituted for creating sounds. Use the instruments to compose, perform, and "harmonize".

MATERIALS: magazines
posterboard/paper
rubber cement
scissors/markers

ACTIVITY: There are two ways to carry out this activity. One way is to copy the following paper doll pattern. The children can color and cut out the dolls. Use the dolls as a pattern to create clothing on separate sheets of construction paper (be sure to include tabs for folding onto the dolls). The second way is to look through magazines or old catalogs. Cut out pictures of people to use as paper dolls. Using rubber cement, glue pictures onto posterboard and cut around the outside of the people. Find pictures of clothes to cut out and place on the paper dolls. Allow free time for the children to play and create conversation using the dolls and clothes.

 Cut pictures for infants. The large paper doll pattern is more desirable when working with infants. Copy, cut and laminate. Prepare clothing. Describe each piece of clothing (color, name, textures). Some older infants may be able to recognize and find objects of clothing when asked (ie: "Where's the sock?").

 Prepare the paper doll in advance for toddlers. Have them find different types of clothes. Ask the children questions about the clothes (ie: "Where do you wear that sock?"). The children can decide the appropriate place for the article of clothing.

Place a piece of paper over the paper doll and the children can design clothes to fit each doll.

CONCEPTS:

- ◆ picture recognition
- ◆ design
- ◆ creative thought
- ◆ color/texture
- ◆ role-playing

VARIATIONS: Use paper dolls and clothes during Creative Play time or Creative Dramatics to enhance language skills, verbal expression, and role-playing. For additional use of magazines, children can cut out favorite pictures and glue onto large pieces of paper. Frame the pictures. Try designing a dream house by cutting different room pictures from magazines. Draw a house outline or blueprint onto a big sheet of paper. Pictures of the rooms can be placed and moved around on the outline to create different layouts of the child's dream house. Use the houses and paper dolls for role-play situations.

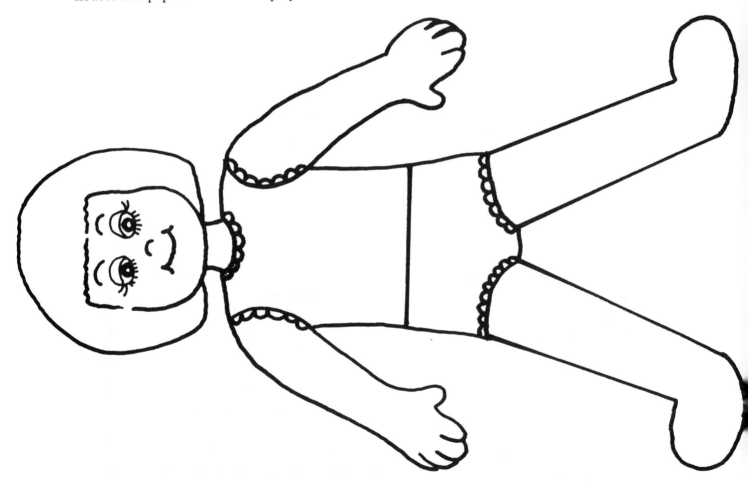

MATERIALS: large blanket
various props

ACTIVITY: Divide into two groups. Each group chooses a familiar story, fairy tale, nursery rhyme, or movie to re-create into a scene. The team decides upon a scene and characters from the chosen story. Two people hold up a blanket while the team sets up the scene (using props is necessary). The team freezes into position, the blanket is dropped, and the other team has to try to guess from what story the scene originated.

 School age children will have to be the organizers and leaders in this activity. Encourage them to get ideas from preschool children and to include toddlers and infants as characters or props.

CONCEPTS:
- ◆ problem-solving
- ◆ creative thought
- ◆ role-playing
- ◆ leadership/cooperation

Pantomiming is very similar to the preceding activity, however, in this exercise, two simple situations will be called aloud. Each child chooses one of these situations and will have a chance to nonverbally create that particular action. No props or words will be used. If the group of children is a little inhibited, then choose one situation at a time for the entire group to perform at once. Here are some fun situations for the younger children to try:

1. Unscrew a light bulb.	10. Jump rope.
2. Feed the dog.	11. Swing a baseball bat.
3. Pour a glass of milk.	12. Be a bride at a wedding.
4. Open a birthday present.	13. Parachute jump.
5. Act like your parents.	14. Be a kernel of corn popping.
6. Be Santa Claus.	15. Mix up a cake.
7. Be a clown juggling.	16. Play a piano (guitar, flute, trumpet).
8. Set the table for lunch.	
9. Crack an egg into a bowl.	17. Be a band leader or drum major.

Below are some fun situations for the older children to try:

> 1. Try to find someone in a crowded train station.
> 2. Save someone from drowning in a pool.
> 3. Wait for a late bus and show your impatience.
> 4. Blow up a balloon, tie it and play.
> 5. Be late for an airplane flight.
> 6. You've just burned yourself while cooking dinner.
> 7. Receive a letter you have been anxiously awaiting for weeks.
> 8. Get into a hot bath and slip on the soap.
> 9. Vacuum the floor and have it start sucking up the curtains.
> 10. Realize you've just won the ten million dollar lottery.
> 11. It is your first time on horseback.
> 12. It is your first singing performance in an auditorium full of people.
> 13. You help a friend move a piano up the stairs.
> 14. You are a famous composer finishing a composition with difficulty.

CONCEPTS:
- ◆ nonverbal communication
- ◆ role-playing/descriptive acting
- ◆ creative thought
- ◆ problem-solving
- ◆ hand/eye/body coordination

MATERIALS: washable markers, chalk or face paint

ACTIVITY: Children paint characters on their hands. Name the characters and discuss their characteristics and personalities. Ask the children to have their characters say some things to the group. Make up stories using their hands as the characters in the story. Play different kinds of music and let the puppets make up their own dances. Encourage children to "dance" to the rhythms, sounds (high-low), and interpret expression and meaning.

 Using each child's hand character, the older children can write a song, choreograph a dance, or write a skit or play involving everyone's hand puppet. They can be the directors and help younger children learn the songs, lines, and roles (remind the school age children to make lines easy and the skits short!). Make a puppet stage to perform.

CONCEPTS:
- ◆ creative thought/ problem solving
- ◆ leadership/rhythm
- ◆ improvisation/ dramatic interpretation

156

Chapter 9:

Learning With Food-Nutrition

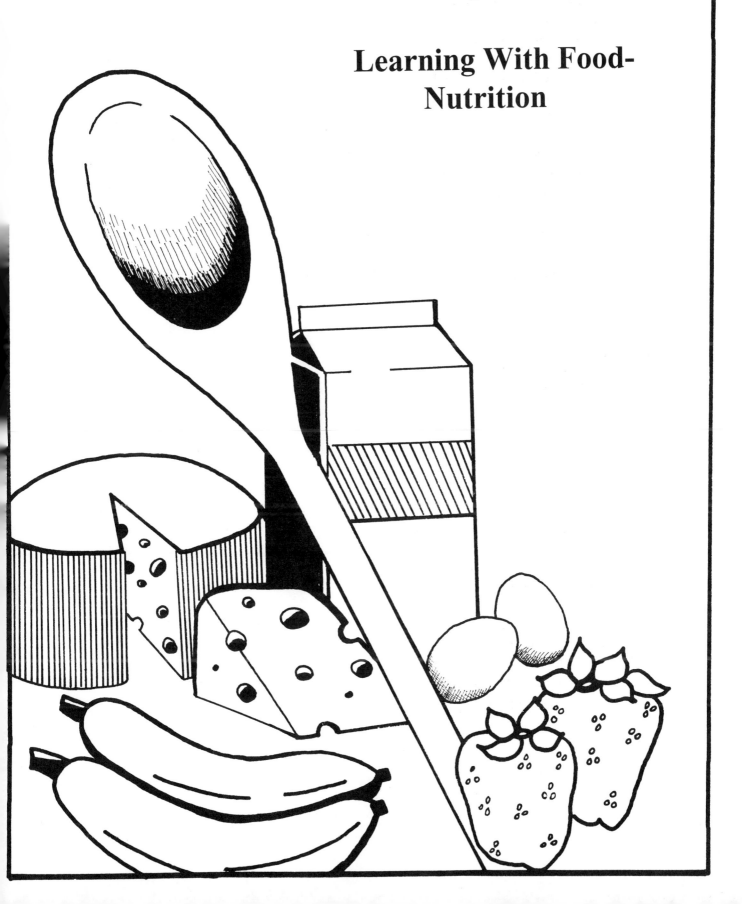

Chapter 9 Introduction

Learning about good nutrition is essential for everyone. With children, using food as a learning tool can be so much fun. From reading a story about Johnny Appleseed to counting raisins to lacing cereal, food can be used in many, many ways. When children learn with food, they can also learn about nutrition and the importance of good health. This chapter will use food in nutritional activities as well as different subject areas.

The following are very simplified descriptions of each food group in the nutritional pyramid. For more detailed information on nutrition, daily requirements per age group, meals, and measurements, contact your local food program representative, health department, or local library.

Fat Group
limit intake of
fats and sweets

Milk Group

milk, cheese, yogurt,
ice cream

Meat Group

meat, poultry, eggs,
soy, nuts

Fruit Group

all fruits and 100 % fruit juices

Vegetable Group

all vegetables and 100 %
vegetable juices

Bread Group

Breads and cereals with first ingredient being a whole grain or enriched grain product
(Pastas, rolls, bagels, buns, rice, pancakes, waffles, etc.- be sure to check labels for
the first ingredient!)

Note: Many of the activities in this chapter have been adapted from publications: "Infants and Toddlers on the Move" and "Kitchen Magic", with permission and courtesy of Wildwood Resources, Inc..

MATERIALS: milk
food coloring
cereal bowl
liquid dish soap

ACTIVITY: Pour milk into the bowl. Add a few drops of food coloring. Place a drop of liquid dish soap on each drop of food coloring. Discuss what happens to the colors. Tell the children that although they cannot see it, milk contains fat, which does not mix with the watery food coloring. When the liquid dish soap touches the milk, it breaks up the drops of fat which then spread out, allowing the food coloring and milk to mix. **Note:** Demonstration for all and discussion for preschool and older.

CONCEPTS:
- ◆ fat
- ◆ problem-solving
- ◆ discussion skills
- ◆ language development

MATERIALS: clean pie tin
paper towel
1 piece of bread
plastic wrap

ACTIVITY: Place a wet paper towel on the pie tin. Put the bread on it and cover with plastic wrap. In a dark place, leave it for a few days. Let the children observe the bread with a magnifying glass or microscope. Have the children predict outcomes of the experiment.. Ask questions, like: "What happened to the bread?" and "Why do you think the bread changed?". After observations and theories, explain about mold. Molds are plant-like bacteria that grow when they find a suitable environment, such as damp bread. Ask how they think this happens. After discussion, explain that in the air, there are tiny, black and green specks called spores (too small for us to see without a microscope). These spores are like seeds for plants called mold. Molds live off some of the foods we like to eat. The spores grow into fuzzy-looking mold plants which are eating the bread. Mention that some medicines (ie: penicillin) come from mold. Tell them is why food goes bad or spoils. **Note:** Demonstration for all, discussion for preschool and older.

CONCEPTS:
- ◆ science experimentation (prediction/outcomes)
- ◆ problem-solving
- ◆ critical thinking skills/ building vocabulary
- ◆ microorganisms

MATERIALS: magazines
paper
scissors/glue

ACTIVITY: Children look through magazines to find pictures of foods that they like to eat. Cut and glue pictures to paper to make books. After completion, practice recognizing the food groups of each picture (refer to the food groups shown earlier in this chapter).

Toddlers can help look through magazines with you. Cut out their favorite foods and let them do the gluing.

Have children find a favorite food in each food group. They can pick one food and research the history of that food. Write a short report to tell the other children.

CONCEPTS:
- ◆ food recognition
- ◆ self-awareness
- ◆ nutritional grouping
- ◆ hand-eye coordination

VARIATION: Design booklet covers for an Arts and Crafts project.

MATERIALS: oranges
fruit salad (cut into small pieces)
marker
knife

ACTIVITY: Cut top off orange and scoop out the insides. Add to fruit salad. Fill the scooped out orange with the fruit. Draw faces on the orange with marker and replace the tops of the oranges. Serve with lunch or add another food from the other food groups for a nutritious snack.

ALL: Be sure older infants are ready for finger food before serving this activity.

CONCEPTS:
- ◆ nutritional value
- ◆ creative thinking

l c. shortening	1/2 tsp. salt
3/4 c. honey	3/4 c. honey
l egg	l c. molasses
5 c. flour	1/2 tsp. salt
l 1/2 tsp. baking soda	l tsp. cinnamon
1 tsp. cloves	

Mix shortening, honey, egg and molasses. Sift soda, salt, spices, and flour. Mix dry ingredients with shortening mixture. Roll out 1/4" thick onto floured surface. Cut with gingerbread man cookie cutters or make a pattern. Bake at 375 degrees for 10 minutes
*This is credited as a bread alternate with a two times a week limit.

All the children will have fun helping with this recipe. Hang the gingerbread men on the tree at Christmas or give as gifts.

VARIATIONS: This can be a follow-up activity after reading "The Gingerbread Man". Have each child make up a character that chases the gingerbread man, dictate a sentence ("I've been chased by _____.") and illustrate the page for Reading. Make gingerbread people and decorate into different career people (ie:; firefighter, doctor, postal worker, etc.) for Social Studies.

MATERIALS: gingerbread man cookie cutter
bread
peanut butter
raisins

ACTIVITY: Cut gingerbread man shapes from white and whole wheat bread. Spread jelly on the backs of the gingerbread men. Place jellied white gingerbread men onto peanut buttered whole wheat bread and vice versa. Use a little peanut butter to fasten raisins onto gingerbread man for eyes, mouth and buttons. While using this project for a snack or lunch, count the raisins as a counting activity.

 Toddlers will need assistance with cutting and spreading.

CONCEPTS:
- ◆ visual discrimination/ food groups recognition
- ◆ fine motor skills

Monster Meringues

4 egg whites
1/8 tsp. cream of tartar
1 tsp. cinnamon
blue food coloring

1 tsp. vanilla
1 c. sifted powdered sugar (or
1 c. and 1 Tbs. sifted sugar)

Preheat oven to 225 degrees. Beat egg whites until foamy. Add cream of tartar and vanilla. Beat, adding sugar one tablespoon at a time until stiff. Drop spoonfuls of mixture on baking sheet. Place in oven for 2 to 2 1/2 hours until firm and dry.

ACTIVITY: Follow the above recipe. Discuss with the children how the meringue forms. When egg whites are whisked, hundred of tiny air bubbles get trapped and make a stiff foam. The oven's heat makes the air bubbles "expand" or enlarge and the foam puffs up. Also, the chemical change in the egg whites makes it solid (this is called coagulation).

 Those infants who are old enough for finger foods and egg whites (not recommended for infants under one year but check with your physician) will love touching the finished product. Put them in a high chair with bibs and allow them to explore the sensations (smell, taste, and touch).

 Although the favorite part of this activity is the touching and tasting, toddlers will enjoy adding pre-measured ingredients to the mixture.

 Children can go exploring in the kitchen to see who can "discover" the most foods that contain air. Help them find and examine items like muffins, breads, bagels, pita bread, and whipped cream.

CONCEPTS:
- air /coagulation
- problem-solving
- language development
- chemical changes
- senses
- nutrition

MATERIALS: A wide selection of different foods (different shapes, sizes and colors).

PREPARATION: Place your collection of foods onto a table or use the following patterns to make food cards.

ACTIVITY: Discuss the food groups. Have children name a food group and take turns picking a food from that group. When they have finished, sort foods into color, size, and shape.

Keep grouping for older infants and toddlers simple but allow children to participate. Watch closely for small objects.

After each grouping, keep records of how many foods belong in each group (Math concepts). Design a chart or graph. Research how some products are marketed.

VARIATION: Discuss the ways in which each food is grown (trees, underground, vines, etc.) for a Science activity. Talk about how some foods are manufactured or processed. Go on a field trip to a dairy, bakery, or other interesting food production place for Social Studies. Use food products as Math manipulatives. Design an ad for a food product as an Arts and Craft project. Write a story using different foods as the characters for Reading and Language Arts. Create a play, songs, and costumes using a food theme or food characters for Music and Drama activities.

CONCEPTS:
- sorting
- food groups
- color/size/shapes
- creative thinking
- language development

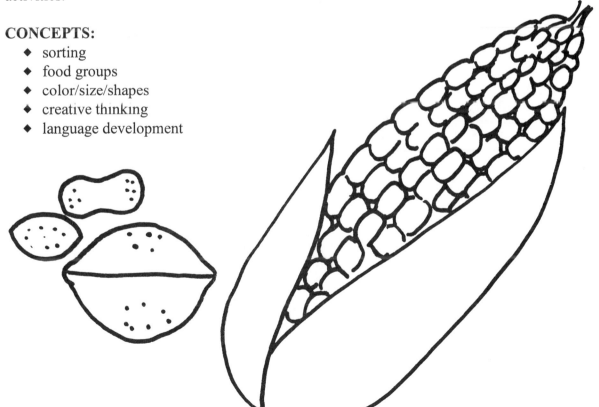

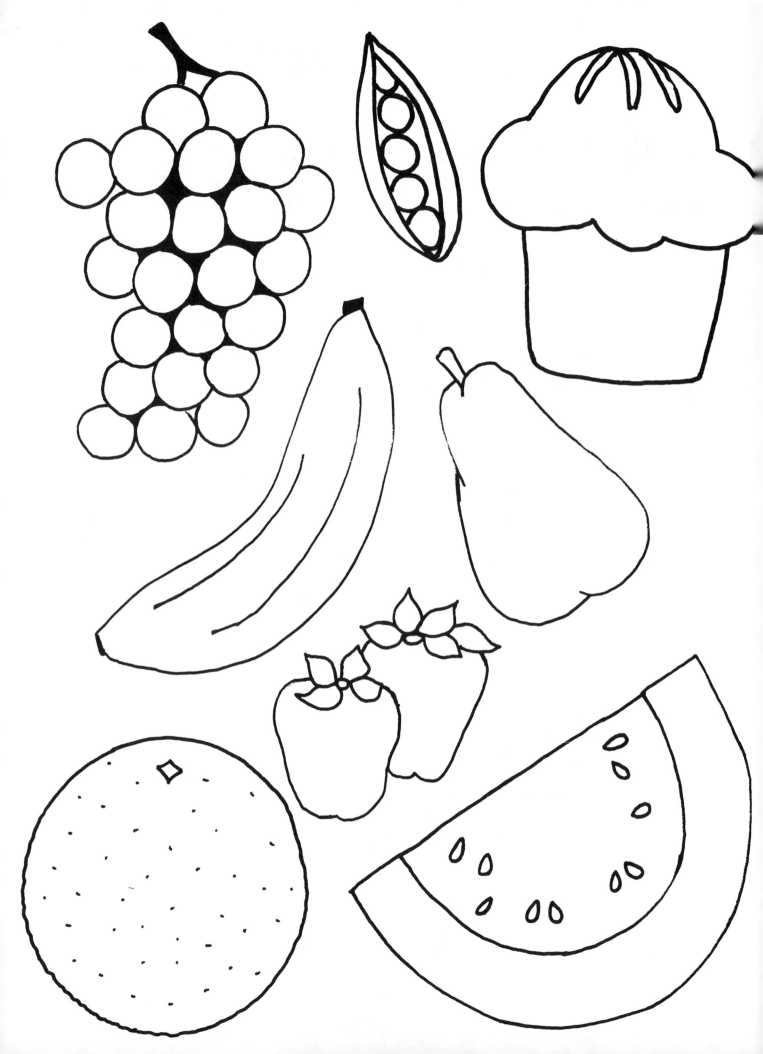

MATERIALS: raisins
sparkling water
juice
glass

PREPARATION: Cut the raisins into small pieces.

ACTIVITY: Place the pieces of raisins into a glass. Pour sparkling water and juice over the pieces and watch the raisins dance! Discuss why the raisins move. The raisins ride on the little bubbles of gas in the sparkling water. The bubbles come to the top, pop, and the raisins sink back to the bottom.

ALL: Everyone can observe the demonstration, but grapes and raisins are **not** recommended for children under age three.

VARIATIONS: Try dropping other types of food (sugar, salt, crackers, etc.) into a similar mixture. Observe, compare, and discuss what happens to each food. This would be a good time to study the raisin (where it comes from and how it is processed). Brainstorm ways in which grapes and raisins are used in different foods and cooking. Have a snack with raisins in it! Draw new "California Raisin" people for an Arts and Crafts project. Use raisins as manipulatives for Math problems. Copy a map of your country and label places where grapes are grown for a Social Studies activity.

CONCEPTS:
- ◆ air
- ◆ raisins/grapes
- ◆ food properties
- ◆ nutrition

Chapter 10:

**Fun for
Everyone-
Creative Play
and
Games**

Chapter 10 Introduction

Playing is an important element in childhood learning at any age. Playing with your children, whether through creative play, group games, store-bought board games, or toys, can help develop trust, self-esteem, and friendship. Objectives for playing include: fine and gross motor development, creative thinking, problem-solving, and social skills development. When you show your enjoyment of the activities, your children will enjoy the learning process. Share this experience of play with your children, and above all, have fun!

Children need to have items to play with that will stimulate their creativity and help them become active. Learning with the use of manipulatives is great "hands on" stimulation for creative thinking. All toys need not be bought in a store. Safe items can be made or collected to use for playing. The following toys are suggested for age appropriateness but use your own judgment. Some children are ready to advance earlier and others like to stick with their "old favorites" longer. Preschool and kindergarten children are developing in the imagination stage.

Preschool and Kindergarten

games	playground	role-playing toys
dolls	equipment	(ie: dishes, play tools,
building blocks	puzzles	medical kits, dress up)
action figures	markers, crayons, paints	puppets

 Toys should be washable, safe, unbreakable, and lightweight. Infants are in an investigative, "put in the mouth" feeling and exploratory stage. Toys should have brightly-colored, exploratory, and kinesthetic qualities.

rattles	balls	wooden puzzles with
stuffed toys	stacking blocks	rounded edges
various sizes/ types	sandboxes with	push toys
containers	shovels and buckets	large pegboards

 Toddlers are in an experimental stage of playing. They will still be showing interest in the infant toys, but are ready for these new play things.

stuffed animals	dolls	building blocks
water/sand toys	puzzles	easy games
plastic people and	riding toys	large plastic cars and
animals	crayons\play dough	trucks

As children begin their school age years, they search for ways to stimulate their active minds and bodies; however, their maturity levels keep them involved with activities that they have known and still enjoy from their preschool and kindergarten years. These toys are suggested to comply with the needs of both worlds.

puppets	**paper dolls**	**playground equipment**
action figures	**skates**	**sports equipment**
bicycles	**paints/craft sets**	**skill games (bowling**
puzzles	**sophisticated doll sets**	**sets, bean tosses,**
scooters	**complex buiding sets**	**safe darts)**
board games		

 As children approach the upper grade school years, their needs become more sophisticated. They enjoy competitive sports, problem-solving board games, collecting (everything!), and more adult-level interaction in their playing. Here are some suggested playing ideas to add to the school age list.

skates/skateboards	**board games**	**hobby sets:**
crafts	**bicycles**	**(stamps, coins, cards,**
playground equipment	**carpentry**	**dolls)**
electrical toys	**difficult puzzles**	**camping/outdoor play**
books	**kites**	

Bingo is an all-time favorite game of the young and old (and in between!). Bing' is similar to Bingo, only it is a homemade game with cards that can be created to reinforce learning skills in various age groups and for various subjects. Copy the sample Bing' card. Create (mix and match) your own Bing' cards using the following category list:

◆ **numbers**	◆ **letters (capital/lower case)**
◆ **pictures (vocabulary)**	◆ **math problems**
◆ **historical figures**	◆ **colors**
◆ **shapes**	◆ **animals**
◆ **plants**	◆ **transportation**
◆ **words**	◆ **famous structures**
◆ **cultural studies**	◆ **foreign languages**

Make the cards as difficult or easy as required for the age group. Cut out one set of squares to match the Bing' cards. The leader picks 1 card, shows or calls the card, and everyone places a button (or blank squares) to cover the matching space on their card if a match is called. Make your own rules on winning (4 matches across, up and down, diagonal, corners, etc.).

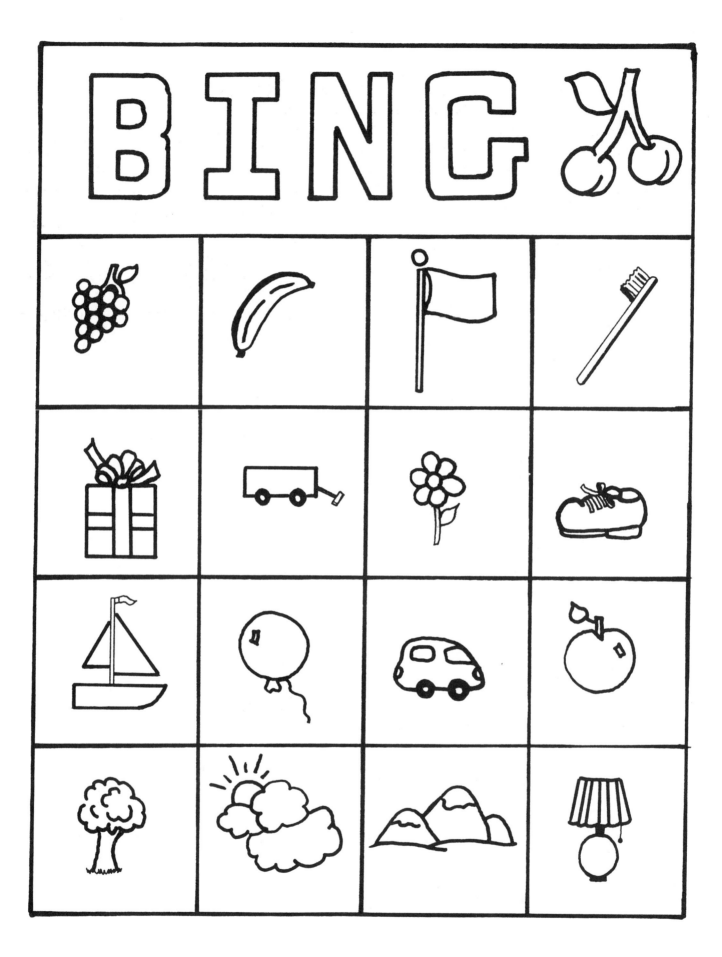

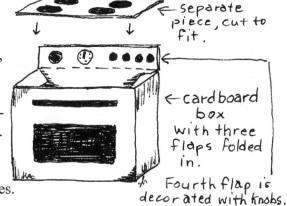

Make A Kitchen

Playing house or kitchen can keep children of all ages (boys and girls alike) busy for long periods of time. So much can be learned as they create situations, develop social skills, recognize responsible behaviors, stimulate their imaginations, and increase self-awareness.

← separate piece, cut to fit.

← cardboard box with three flaps folded in.

Fourth flap is decorated with knobs.

Design your own housekeeping area by making home-made stoves, refrigerators, sinks, cupboards, and microwaves. Use large boxes for large items. Smaller boxes can be used to design toasters, coffee makers, blenders, and other small appliances. Extremely large boxes can be used to make playhouses. Cut out doors and decorate with paint. Be sure the kids are involved in design and decoration.

Refrigerator from box

Save empty non-glass containers and boxes. Fill your housekeeping area with a play ironing board, table, blankets, brooms, dolls, dress up clothes, dishes, and anything else that is safe and fits into the theme.

VARIATION: Save same sized cereal boxes (you'll need a lot of them!). Build a house using the cereal boxes as blocks. Glue together using a hot glue gun. Be sure to leave spaces for windows and a door. Be creative!

It's A Puzzle

MATERIALS: calendar pictures
lightweight cardboard (8" x 10")
rubber cement
scissors

ACTIVITY: Glue pictures to cardboard with rubber cement or decoupage paste (regular white glue buckles the pictures). Cut pictures with scissors or allow older children to use a razor knife). Make cuts more difficult for older children and simpler for younger children. Keep puzzle pieces in a ziplock bag for future play.

Sometimes children have a difficult time deciding what they want to play. They may be calling out to you for a little more structure or some suggestions. When this happens, it is time to set up a center rotation. Each activity during center time can be called a center or a station. Set up activities or play areas around a large room. Have equal amount of play areas for the number of children who will be participating. If you have six children, set up six areas of play. Here is an example:

CENTERS/STATIONS

1. **play dough** - a small lump of dough at a table with a few playing utensils
2. **lacing beads** - string and beads
3. **building blocks** - any kind that are age appropriate, preferably on a floor area
4. **painting** - piece of paper, watercolors, water
5. **puzzles** - set out two for each age group
6. **listening/reading** - set up a tape player with books on tape or place several books out for reading along with a bean bag chair or pillow.

Stations can be anything you have on hand, a planned activity, specific toy, craft, game, and so on. After the stations have been set up, assign a child to each station (number each station and have them "draw" numbers to see who goes where first). Set a timer for ten minute intervals. When the time is up, rotate the children in a clockwise manner (younger children will need assistance in which station to go to next) and set the timer for another ten minutes. Keep rotating in ten minute intervals until everyone has been to each station. The children love center rotation and may even insist the process be repeated (however, it is best to save it again for another day so they do not burn out on the whole idea).

Some of the most fun times for children and families are times spent playing games together. Little do children realize just how many skills are involved and how much learning can be accomplished while they are having so much fun! Here is a reference list of games on the market and some of the skills that are reinforced or learned by playing them:

◆ READ MY LIPS, JR. (Pressman): ages 8+ * reading, language, social interaction

◆ PICTIONARY JR.: school age * art, language, problem-solving

◆ MICKEY LOOK AND FIND (Parker Brothers): ages 3-6 * social studies, geography

◆ SORRY (Parker Brothers): ages 6+ * counting, number recognition, strategy

- GO TO THE HEAD OF THE CLASS (Milton Bradley): ages 8+ * all areas of educational subjects

- MONOPOLY JR (Parker Brothers): ages 5-8 * math computation, sequencing, counting, money, problem-solving

- MONOPOLY (Parker Brothers): ages 8+ * problem-solving, money, finance, strategy, computation

- LABYRINTH (Cardinal): ages 3+ * hand-eye coordination, motor skills

- KOOSH BASKETBALL (Oddz On): ages 2+ * hand-eye coordination, large motor skills

- LIFE (Milton Bradley): ages 9+ * social skills, counting, money, problem-solving

- RISK/CASTLE RISK: ages 10+ * world and European geography, strategy

- WHERE IN THE WORLD IS CARMEN SAN DIEGO? (University Games): ages 10+ * history, geography

- BATTLESHIP (Milton Bradley): ages 8+ *critical thinking, problem-solving, reasoning

- UNO (International Games): ages 7+ * counting, matching, colors, numbers

- UNO JR. (International Games): preschool 1 * color recognition, counting

- SKIP BO (Mattel): ages 7+ * strategy, numbers strategy, numbers

- ROOK (Parker Brothers): ages 6+ * number and letter recognition

- NERF PRO HOOP (Parker Brothers): ages 2+ * hand-eye coordination, large motor skills

- BOGGLE (Parker Brothers): ages 8+ * reading, language, problem-solving

- BOGGLE JR. (Parker Brothers): ages 4-8 * letters, beginning sounds, visual matching

- YAHTZEE (Milton Bradley): ages 8+ * problem-solving, critical thinking, numbers, math computation

- MICKEY MOUSE YAHTZEE JR. (Milton Bradley): ages 5+ * graphing, counting, matching, problem-solving

- CLUE (Parker Brothers): ages 8+ * deductive reasoning, problem-solving

- CLUE JR. (Parker Brothers): ages 6-10 * reading, problem-solving, counting

- CHECKERS: ages 7+ * problem-solving, strategy

- SNAPSHOT (Cadaco): ages 6+ * visual discrimination, creative thought, problem-solving, number recognition

- RIVERS, ROADS AND RAILS (Ravensburger): ages 4+ * matching, discrimination, visual skills

- EARLY DISCOVERIES (Discovery Toys): ages 3+ * colors, visual skills, counting, matching, problem-solving

- MIDNIGHT PARTY (Ravensburger): ages 8+ * strategy, math computation, estimation

- LIGHT N' LEARN (Milton Bradley): ages 3-6 * all areas of preschool education

- GUESS WHO? (Milton Bradley): ages 6+ * descriptive vocabulary, reasoning/deduction, verbalization, picture recognition, problem-solving

These are just some of the store bought games that are on the market today. The following games in this chapter do not require purchasing, but may require a bit of ingenuity.

This game is great with a group of preschool children. Name a color. Have the children race to touch an object in the room that is that color, or has the color in it. If scoring is desired, give points for the first person to touch the correct color. Keep naming different colors and score accordingly. This game can also be played using shapes.

Have a timer, paper, and pencils handy. Name a color and have them write down as many items as they can of that color until the timer goes off (five minutes is a good guideline). Whoever has the most items on her/ his list for each color wins.

Give each child a spoon to hold. Set a ping pong ball on the spoon. Have them walk from a starting point to a finish line. If their balls fall off, the children can pick them up and replace them onto the spoon. This is just for fun, not competition. Rolling ping pong balls on the ground with your nose is also a fun way to play this game. With larger groups of children, teams can be organized to form relay races.

Older children can use ping pong paddles with balls to see how many times they can hit the ball up in the air while standing in one place.

Gather items that have distinctive or unusual textures. Put all these items into a large, opaque plastic or cloth sack. Give each child a chance to grab into the bag and hold one item without bringing the object into visibility. Encourage the child to describe the object and then make a guess as to what the object is. The child can then show the object to see if the guess was correct. Each child will want a turn (or many turns!). Continue until the children become disinterested. Find simpler items for young children and more challenging items for older ones.

"Follow Me" is another name for "Follow the Leader." You be the leader first to show how the game is played. Have the children line up behind you. Start by walking, then run, hop, skip, act like an animal, swing your arms, and so on. Think of as many large or fine motor actions as possible to keep the children's interest. Then allow the child behind you to take your place as leader and you can get at the end of the line. Continue the game until everyone has had a chance to be the leader.

Form a circle on the floor. Say a word to the children and have each child give a name that rhymes with that word. Count how many words rhyme with the original word. Give each child a chance to say a word for the rest of the group. Keep the game going until all the children have had a turn to say a word. Explain that rhyming words are words that have endings that sound the same. Allow the children to mime (act out) the rhyming words, if desired.

MATERIALS: 4" x 6" cards

PREPARATION: Write numbers 1 through 10 onto the cards. Have the children sit in a circle on the floor. Give each child a number card. Do not let anyone else see the numbers.

GAME: Have each child look at their own number. On the signal "go," the children hold their cards up for everyone to see. After about three seconds, signal the children to hide their cards behind their backs. Each child then gets a turn to choose a person in the circle and try to guess the number that person is holding. If they guess correctly, they can keep that person's card.

Take turns guessing around the circle until each child has had a turn. For younger children, use picture cards with familiar objects, instead of numbers.

Below are a few extra "game" ideas specifically for infants. The other children can play, too!

1. **Mirrors** - Set infants in front of a mirror and watch them play! Safe reflective toys can be found to set around very young infants while they lie on the floor, playpen, or crib.

2. **Peek A Boo** - All babies love hiding games. Get a blanket, cover yourself up, and then show yourself. Hide a puppet or other toys or objects. Have those objects show up in different places from under the blanket. The infant tries to locate where the object is "peeking" out.

3. **Nursery Rhymes** - Set the infant on your lap facing you. Bounce the child lightly while reciting a favorite nursery rhyme. (If you are not familiar or do not remember any from childhood, the library is full of nursery rhyme picture books!)

4. **Copy Me!** - Make sounds, faces, or other actions. Try to get the infant to copy you. Be happy and enjoy playing with your infant.

5. **Hide and Seek** - Hide an object in the room (or hide yourself so you are invisible to the infant) Ask the child "Where is the...?" or "Where am I?" Younger infants will look around and older infants will crawl or even walk to seek you or the object.

There are many objects that can be used when creating tossing games. Bean bags, balls (Nerf balls are best for indoors), rings, and small stuffed animals are a few tossable items. Homemade bean bags are easy to make and economical, too. Just cut two equal squares (approximately 6"). Sew a one-inch seam around the outside of the squares, leaving a couple of inches open to fill the bags. Fill with beans and sew up the opening.

Waste baskets, buckets, hoola hoops, tote trays, bins, and paper sacks are some suggested targets. Rules of the tossing games can be made up by you or the children. Use tape on the floor to designate different starting points for older infants, toddlers, preschoolers, and school age children. Decide upon how many throws, scoring (if any), and ways to toss (overhand, under the leg, backwards, blindfolded, underhand, etc.).

CONCEPTS:
- ◆ creative thinking
- ◆ large motor skills
- ◆ hand-eye coordination
- ◆ problem-solving

Paper Punching Bag

When a child is angry or frustrated, he or she sometimes lashes out at other children nearby. This activity can redirect inappropriate behavior and turn it into positive playing.

MATERIALS: paper bags (sturdy)
markers
string

ACTIVITY: Allow the children to decorate their bags using markers. If desired, reinforce a theme for decorating the bags. Fill the bags with crumpled up newspaper and tie the bag closed with a string. Hang the bags from a doorway or ceiling and allow the children to "punch" out their frustrations on the bags.

CONCEPTS:
- creativity
- feelings
- self-image
- problem-solving

Stringing Stuff

Stringing, lacing and creating jewelry can definitely be considered an arts and crafts type of activity, but it can also be included in creative play. Stringing is similar to building with blocks. The children keep adding items until they obtain a final result, then take it apart and start again to create an entirely different item. Here are some suggested materials to put into a "stringing" bucket of play:

buttons	**beads**
hoops	**wooden shapes (with**
washers	**holes)**
rubber bands	**jar rubbers**
glazed cereals	**rings**
keys	**spools**

Browse through a craft store to find numerous types of items that can be strung. Be sure there is a variety to keep on hand to put into the bucket. Use shoelaces or other string type materials for the stringing (The tips of the strings should have a coating so they do not fray). The children are then ready to create and play. This is an age appropriate activity, so beware of tiny parts with younger children.

MATERIALS: white thick paper or lightweight cardboard
carbon paper
hole puncher
markers/crayons
old shoe strings

PREPARATION: Find pictures from coloring books, magazines, old picture books, or calendars. Trace or draw pictures, or have the children design their own pictures.

ACTIVITY: Children can color their pictures. When finished, laminate pictures. Punch holes around the outside of the pictures. Children lace their pictures and keep them to play with another day.

CONCEPTS:
- fine motor skills
- hand-eye coordination
- creative thought

Using any household items, set up a maze for kids indoors! Lay the ropes (jump-ropes are fine) on the floor. Set up chairs, boxes, toys and other objects. Have children run through the maze. Make up a beginning and end to the maze. Change the activity by having children crawl, hop, walk, or go backwards.

CONCEPTS:
- large motor skills
- action perceptions
- spatial relationships
- following directions

VARIATION: This activity can also be accomplished by setting up an obstacle course. Instead of the children walking through a maze, have them climb over, jump over, crawl under, walk on, etc...

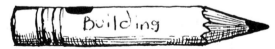

Building is an important part of playing and learning. Keep plenty of building blocks and building type toys on hand. Here are a few "homemade" ideas to add to the collection:

HOMEMADE BLOCKS

Use scrap pieces of wood or buy cheap wood from a local craft store. Sand and treat with a **child safe** paint or finish. Store in an empty bin or tub container.

PAPER BUILDING

Save old scraps of construction paper left over from previous craft projects. Store them in an old shoebox. Cut scraps into squares, circles, rectangles, triangles, and other shapes. Children can "build" on paper by placing shapes onto a large piece of paper. These shapes can be arranged to make pictures or designs. If desired, pictures can become finalized by gluing them onto a large piece of background paper.

ODDS AND ENDS

Save pie tins, playing cards, milk cartons, paper cups, fast food containers, plastic containers, and any other containers that could be used in building. Store items in a large bucket or laundry basket. Odds and ends give children new and creative ways of problem-solving and building.

MATERIALS: old gloves
scrap materials
craft eyes

ACTIVITY: Cut off the ends of the fingers on a pair of old gloves. Children can glue on decorations, eyes, hair, and other accessories to create finger puppet characters.

CONCEPTS:
- ◆ creative thinking
- ◆ problem-solving
- ◆ role-playing

VARIATION: Make a small stage from a shoebox so children can create their own finger puppet shows.

Plastic and cardboard lids can be found every day in most homes, and they are an extremely inexpensive source of fun. Since they are mostly non-recyclable, reusing them in an educational program or for playing is the ideal method of 'disposal'.

 l. Infants and toddlers will thrill at touching, stacking and tasting different sized and shaped lids. Collect safe and sturdy lids to keep in an old container or plastic bucket.

 2. Using a sharp razor knife, cut out stencil forms for children to practice tracing and recognizing. Make a set of letters, numbers and shapes.

3. Paint pictures on lids to reinforce picture recognition of animals, objects, types of transportation, flowers, food, and other subjects.

4. Use the lids for building materials or for making sculptures.

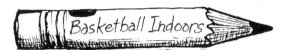

Set up a wastebasket and use wadded paper or foil, wadded up socks, round foam rubber balls, or any item that is safe and resembles a basketball. Have a basketball game with all ages. Make up rules and scoring according to age groups and skills. Try new ways to play, such as: crawl instead of run, shoot blindfolded, hop on one leg to the basket, shoot backwards, shoot with feet instead of hands, and so on. The crazier the game, the more fun it becomes!

Using wooden blocks or any other desired building materials you have on hand, set up a bowling alley right in your home or school! Place any number of blocks up in any shape desired (be creative!). Use a rubber ball or kickball to roll for knocking over the blocks. Create your own games, rules, scoring, and materials according to skill levels.

There are many ways memory games can be set up and played. The older the group, the more items can be added to remember. Gather small items from the house to put onto a cookie sheet. Let the children examine the items for three minutes. See how many items the children can remember from the tray. The game can also be played by removing one item and showing the tray to see if they can recognize which item is missing. Start with three items for toddlers and work your way up. Have older children make a list of what they saw and compare with the tray of items after a time limit has been met. Preschoolers and kindergartners can draw pictures of the remembered items and compare notes after time is up. Another variation of the game is to remove or add something from one particular room and have the children try to guess what is missing or what is new.

Find items that make sounds (bells, sticks, musical instruments, sandpaper, crumpled paper, etc.). There are also some very good sound effects cassette tapes that can be purchased inexpensively at discount stores. Have children sit facing away from you on the floor. Make noises or play sound effect tapes. Children try to guess each noise that is made. Give them the chance to be the leader and make certain sounds for the other children and you to guess.

180

Going On A Trip

Now here is one of those old favorite road trip games that used to keep traveling families entertained for hours. Start the game with one person saying, "I'm going on a trip and I'm going to bring..." that person names an item (example: a toothbrush). The next person says, "I'm going on a trip and I'm going to bring a toothbrush and a nightgown." The next person says, "I'm going on a trip and I'm going to bring a toothbrush, a nightgown, and a bathing suit." The game keeps on going with the list of items growing until one person cannot remember. That person is eliminated and the game continues until there is a winner. This game is best with older children and adults but younger children can participate by helping you think of items for the list.

VARIATIONS: This game is a great way to reinforce lessons within your themes. For example, your theme is "The Wild West". Instead of saying "I'm going on a trip..", the game would start with: "I'm a cowboy (or cowgirl) and I need a set of spurs". The game would continue by adding on to the list of things used by people in the old west. The same game can be played with a Circus theme (what people in the circus use), a World theme (what people would pack from other countries), a Farm theme (items farmers need) and so on.

Point To...

"Point to..." is a game that parents probably play with their older infants and toddlers without even classifying it as a "game". Simply ask the children to point to different objects in a room or specific items organized ahead of time. This game is good for vocabulary building, language skills, and listening. Simple praise is the only scoring necessary with this game. Make the game more difficult by pointing to an item and asking "What is this?" Then it becomes the "What is This?" game!

Simon Says

Simon Says is another one of those "old favorites." But as with many "old favorites", it's fun to change them to create new ideas. For toddlers and preschoolers, the game can be played as if it were a simple "Follow the Leader" game. The leader says "Simon Says" on every command and the children copy without being eliminated. One variation is "Simon On Paper", where the children must draw certain objects, letters, or numbers in certain locations; for example, "Simon Says, put a star in the top left corner, then draw a circle under the star." Another variation is to use playdough to play a new version of Simon Says. Each child sits at a table with a chunk of playdough. The leader gives commands to do something with or to the playdough (ie: "Simon Says poke three holes into the playdough", "Simon Says make a ball", etc.). Think of new ways to make an old game exciting.

Make a list of items around the house or outside items. Here are a few list ideas:

• clothespins	• dirty sock	• pine cone
• napkins	• rubber band	• pretzel
• blade of grass	• fly swatter	• scrap of material
• ladybug	• purple sweater	• paper clip
• dandelion	• thread	• rock

For older children, give them each their own list and a sack to gather the items. See who can find the most items on their lists in a certain length of time. Make lists different or the same. For younger children who cannot read, draw pictures or name items on the list for them to gather.

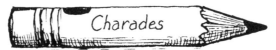

Charades, played by two teams, is an acting out game that can have many rules and actions. Most people have played a game of charades at least once. Older children and adults can find the intricate details in a book of rules and actions from the local library. For preschool and young school-age children, write actions or draw pictures on a small piece of paper. Fold each one up and put them into a bowl. Have one child choose a piece of paper. Whisper into their ear what is on their paper if they cannot recognize it. The child then has three minutes to "act out" the item or action that is on his/her paper. The other children try to guess. The correct guesser and the actor each get a point and the game continues with a new actor.

MATERIALS: paper towel tube
1 foot of string
plastic lid

PREPARATION: Attach string with staples to the end of a tube. Cut out a circle from a plastic lid. Attach the lid the other end of the string.

GAME: Children can try to get the end of the tube into the ring. Practice counting how many times they make a ringer. Be sure each child has a tube ring of her own. Conduct races to see who can get the ring on the tube first.

182

Take turns blindfolding the children and let a partner guide that child around the house. The blindfolded child feels objects and tries to guess what they are. Partners switch places and the game continues. This game can be played in the backyard or at a park to create summer fun. All age groups will enjoy testing their kinesthetic skills (It is doubtful that very young children will allow you to put a blindfold on them, so just try having them close their eyes!). **Use safety precautions when blindfolding children.**

Each child finds or brings a newborn photo of themselves. Do not allow anyone else to see the pictures. Gather the children into a circle on the floor. Hold up a picture and give each child a chance to guess the person in the picture. After each child has a turn, remove the pictures that have been guessed correctly. If there are pictures left, go around the circle again. It is also fun to add a few other baby pictures that the children may not recognize (neighbors, parents, friends, other relatives).

Be sure to add all the large motor games and activities to the playing arena! Physical activity is essential to healthy and happy children (and adults!). Make up relay races or have children create their own. Create new Tag games using TV characters, comic characters, movies, book titles, foods, and other subjects (the person who is "it" runs to tag someone, unless they can call out a name of a movie, food, book title, and so forth).

Hopscotch, jump roping (there are hundreds of ways and rhymes for this), and wheeled items (bicycles, skateboards, roller-skates, wagons, scooters, etc.) are favorite large motor activities. Make up games to play on playground equipment (Follow the Leader is fun when there are jungle gyms). Never forget all the ball games the children love to play. Kickball, soccer, basketball, dodgeball, softball, and other ball games can easily fit into your program.

Children also love to exercise, especially to music. Make up your own kids' aerobic workout or buy exercise tapes for kids. Go for walks together, put on some music to free-style dance, or encourage gymnastic type floor activities (ie: somersaults, cartwheels, and so on). Large motor development is very important for growing bodies and minds!

Chapter 11:

Holiday Celebrations

Chapter 11 Introduction

Holidays can be hectic times during the year for child care professionals or parents, but holiday themes are very useful teaching tools. Designing craft ideas, building integrated study units, and creating activities around holidays make planning fun and easy. This chapter is full of creative learning experiences beginning with major holiday activities in order of their yearly occurrence. Following major holiday plans, find gift ideas to make for special occasions and additional activities for all occasions. Use your favorite craft individually or create entire lessons around one of the activities. One word of advice when planning; use caution not to over-do the holiday themes or begin too early because the excitement of the holiday may over-stimulate the children or wear out the magic. Just enjoy the magic; holidays are very special times for children.

WINTER

MATERIALS: white construction paper
black marker
string
scissors/pencil

PREPARATION: Fold paper in half three times. Open the paper and fold it in a fan-like manner. Copy the snowman pattern onto the folded paper.

ACTIVITY: Children cut snowmen out on the dotted lines. Open the paper and lay the strand of snowmen on a table. Decorate with eyes, noses, and buttons made from paper, colored markers, or glitter. Using glue around the edges, attach each half snowman to the one next to it until a three-sided snowman is formed. Staple string to snowmen and hang.

 Hang snowmen where babies can enjoy. Talk to the child about snowmen, using descriptive words (ie: cold, white, round, happy).

 Cut children's snowmen and have them do their own decorating.

Older children can prepare the entire project. Children can make different types of snowmen and use them as mobiles.

CONCEPTS:
- ◆ fine motor skills/folding
- ◆ following directions
- ◆ dimension

VARIATIONS: Begin activity with a story about snow or a snowman for Reading. Conduct a science experiment by gathering snow in cups and time the rate of melting. Chart the results. Discuss all aspects of snow.

MATERIALS: white construction paper
black or blue paper
glue

ACTIVITY: Children rip pieces of white paper and "build" a snowman by gluing ripped paper onto the dark colored paper. Smaller pieces of ripped paper can be used for a "snowing" effect on the picture.

 Help older infants and toddlers by "drawing" a snowman shape with the glue. The children can rip and sprinkle pieces of paper onto the glue.

GROUNDHOG DAY

MATERIALS: paper
popsicle sticks
glue
paper cups
scissors

PREPARATION: Copy the following groundhog pattern.

ACTIVITY: The children can color their groundhogs, cut, and glue them onto the top of a popsicle stick. Make slits into the bottom of each paper cup. Slide the bottom end of the stick into the slit through the cup opening. After discussing the meaning of Groundhog Day (if the groundhog sees his shadow and hides, that means there will be six more weeks of winter), the children can create make-believe predictions with their very own groundhogs.

Play with the groundhog puppet with infants ("Peek a Boo, Mr. Groundhog!" is a perfect game at this age). Toddlers can color and glue their own puppets.

CONCEPTS:
- ◆ animal behavior
- ◆ customs/ folklore/ weather
- ◆ fine motor skills
- ◆ creativity/ role playing

VARIATIONS: Research the ways in which weather is predicted today. Draw pictures or set up a weather station for a Science activity. For Math, introduce graphing techniques by graphing each child's groundhog prediction, or graph the weather for a week. Read stories about weather and seasons.

(bow optional)

paws → dirty from digging

VALENTINES DAY

Valentine Pups

MATERIALS: white, red, pink and black paper
scissors
glue
heart pattern

PREPARATION: Draw hearts using the patterns.
Enlarge or shrink the patterns for desired sizes.

ACTIVITY: Cut hearts using any
combination of colors desired. Glue hearts
together to form a puppy as shown.

bone

 Give older infants different sizes of colored hearts. Ask them to hand you hearts.
Describe the hearts to them while you glue the puppies together for them.

 Cut hearts for the children and go through the gluing process step by step
(see Chapter 2), asking toddlers to select different sizes. See if they can determine
placement of each heart.

 Give children many varieties of sizes and colored hearts to create other Valentine
creatures or pets.

CONCEPTS:
- ◆ creative thought
- ◆ fine motor skills
- ◆ size differentiation
- ◆ color contrast

VARIATION: Make Valentine worms
using different colored hearts as patterns for Math.

Tissue Fluff Hearts

MATERIALS: red tagboard
pink or red tissue paper, cut into 2" squares
glue
scissors

PREPARATION: Draw a large heart onto tagboard.

ACTIVITY: Children wrap tissue squares around the tip of their finger or on the eraser end of a pencil and dip into glue. Press squares onto the heart. Decorate the entire red hearts with tissue paper puffs.

CONCEPTS:
- ◆ shape recognition
- ◆ fine motor skills
- ◆ creative thought

MATERIALS: construction paper
old crayons
waxed paper
newspaper
iron
tape/ grater

PREPARATION: Grate old crayons to make colored shavings. Use Valentine colors .Fold two pieces of construction paper in half and draw a large heart as shown in the diagram. Cut a piece of waxed paper twice the size of the construction paper.

ACTIVITY: Children cut out the hearts. Fold the piece of waxed paper in half. Spread crayon shavings inside the folded waxed paper to make a design. After placing newspapers on an ironing board, carefully lay waxed paper with shavings on top. Cover with a layer of newspapers and iron. The crayons melt together to form beautiful colors. Cool completely before taping the design between the two outside areas of construction paper (with the heart hole). Tape together.

Note: The ironing part of this activity is not recommended for young children. Older children should have adult supervision at all times.

CONCEPTS:
- ◆ fine motor skills
- ◆ melting
- ◆ temperature
- ◆ design/color

It is easy to pick up a box of Valentines for the children to pass out to their friends, but sometimes it is more fun and special to give a few homemade cards, too. Here are a few suggestions to make Valentine cards more special:

POTATO PRINT HEARTS

Cut a potato in half and carve a heart shape from the flat side. Place a sponge into a bowl and pour paint onto the sponge. Press the potato print onto the paint and print designs onto a folded piece of construction paper. After drying, write a poem or message inside.

SPONGE PRINTS

Cut sponges into shapes (hearts, teddy bears, flowers). Dip sponges into paint and print onto folded construction paper. Write a Valentine message inside the card after drying.

REVERSAL HEART CUT OUTS

Fold a piece of construction paper in half and cut out several hearts on the fold. Open the folded paper and glue onto another piece of construction paper to get an outlined heart effect.

DOILY HEART CARDS

Buy paper doilies from a craft store. Cut several hearts from construction paper and glue onto the doilies, or cut hearts from the doilies and glue onto the paper. Write messages onto the hearts.

MAGAZINE/OLD CARD CUT OUTS

Cut large hearts from construction paper. Using special magazine pictures or pictures cut from old greeting cards, glue pictures onto the paper hearts. Write dialogue or messages around the pictures.

GLITTERY SWEET CARDS

Fold square pieces of tagboard to desired card size. On the front of the card, children can make patterns by gluing conversational hearts and red hot heart candies. On the inside, glue a message and glitter.

PRESIDENT'S DAY

Thinkin' Lincoln

MATERIALS: black construction paper
white paper
white crayon
scissors
glue

PREPARATION: On black paper, use the white crayon to draw an enlarged silhouette pattern of Lincoln.

ACTIVITY: Cut silhouettes and glue them to white paper.

CONCEPTS:
- ◆ historical significance
- ◆ Abraham Lincoln/Civil War
- ◆ abstract art
- ◆ silhouettes

VARIATIONS: Read a story about Lincoln to the children for Social Studies. Count Lincoln pennies for a Math project. Trace outlines of each child to make individual silhouettes for Arts and Crafts. Discuss and experiment with shadows and light to reinforce Science concepts. Write a skit about Lincoln and perform it for Creative Dramatics. Have children dictate a sentence about Lincoln to write under the silhouette and make a big book with all the pages.

 Write a story about life during Lincoln's time. Read about the Civil War and draw pictures. Using the letters in Lincoln's name, have children think of words to describe his character or appearance.

Stovepipe Hats

MATERIALS: large black construction paper
white crayon
scissors
stapler/glue

PREPARATION: Use a white crayon to draw circles on a piece of black paper. Cut out the middle circle.

ACTIVITY: Children cut the outer circle and tabs. Roll large paper into a cylinder the size of each head. Fold and glue tabs to the underside of the rim. Read a story about Abe Lincoln and discuss the meaning of presidency.Research the stovepipe hat and write a short article about how and when it was created.

hat brim

crown

cut out

glue or tape to form cylinder

CONCEPTS:
- ◆ historical significance
- ◆ fine motor skills
- ◆ language development

VARIATIONS: Draw 3" pictures of stovepipe hats onto construction paper. With a white crayon, write numbers on each hat. Children can put hats into numerical order for a Math activity. Creative Dramatics is fun if you add the stovepipe hat to a variety of other hats and allow the children to role-play different characters. Have children dictate stories and illustrate pictures about what they think it means to be President. Put the stories and pictures together to make a book for Reading.

MATERIALS: green/brown construction paper
red paint/brushes
scissors
large piece newsprint

ACTIVITY: Children trace their hands onto green paper and cut along the outlines. Cut a tree trunk from the brown paper. Glue hands and trunk onto the large piece of newsprint to form a tree. Paint cherries on the leaves. After the project is completed, read a story about young George Washington and the cherry tree. Remind the children that "chopping down the cherry tree" is only a story that has been passed down over the years.

CONCEPTS:
- ◆ historical significance
- ◆ fine motor skills

VARIATIONS: Make ten hand prints and paint one cherry on one, two on one and so on. Children can count the cherries on each tree to reinforce counting skills for Math. Talk about trees and plants for Science. Visit a tree farm. Bake a cherry pie or dessert for a Nutrition activity.

ST. PATRICK'S DAY

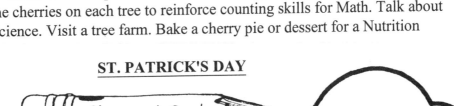

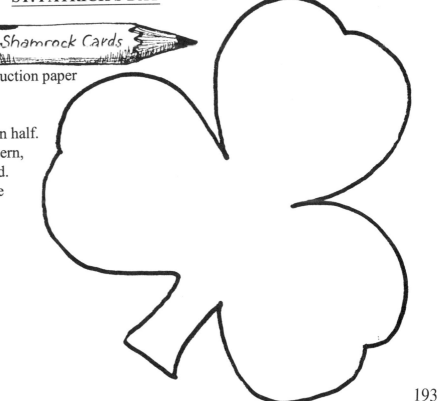

MATERIALS: green construction paper
scissors

ACTIVITY: Fold paper in half. Using the following shamrock pattern, trace and cut shamrocks on the fold. Here are just a few limericks to use inside your shamrock cards!

> **Roses are red,**
> **Shamrocks are green**
> **You are the best (mom,**
> **dad, sister...)**
> **I've ever seen!**

MATERIALS: paper
scissors/glue
yarn
crayons or markers

PREPARATION: Draw the leprechaun mask
from the pattern.

ACTIVITY: Discuss St. Patrick's Day and where the Irish custom came from (get a
book from the library). Read your favorite leprechaun picture book then follow up the lesson
with cutting, coloring, and decorating the masks.

CONCEPTS:
- customs
- geography
- creative thought
- fine motor skills

VARIATIONS: Locate Ireland on the globe and continue cultural studies of the country for
Social Studies. Have the children dictate stories about their leprechauns for Reading.

EASTER

MATERIALS: eggs
paints/brushes
glitter
glue
dried flowers
3" x 3" pieces of wood

PREPARATION: Blow eggs out of shells by poking a small hole in each end of an egg (eggs
should be warmed to room temperature) and blowing carefully on one end of the egg. Rinse well
with soap and water.

ACTIVITY: Paint or glitter eggs with designs. Glue eggs onto small blocks of wood.
Arrange dried flowers around egg and glue into place.

VARIATIONS: Find a book about holiday customs. Research how the egg first became an
Easter custom (to use as a basis for Social Studies concepts). Read a story about the Easter
Bunny and make an alphabet egg with painted letters to reinforce letter recognition in the
Reading Program.

Leprechaun pattern

punch hole for string →

punch hole for other end of string

Papier Mâché Eggs

MATERIALS: strips of newspaper
flour/water
balloons
paint/brushes

PREPARATION: Blow up balloons and cover work area with newspapers (see Chapter 2 for papier mache instructions and recipe).

ACTIVITY: Dip strips of newspaper into paste and slide two fingers down strips to remove excess paste. Smooth strip around balloon. Continue process until the balloon is covered with several layers. Allow to dry. Paint decorations onto the egg.

ALL

CONCEPTS:
- creative thought
- hand-eye coordination
- shapes

Marshmallow Bunnies

MATERIALS: paper/felt
large and mini marsh-
mallows or jelly beans
glue
Easter grass
toothpicks

ACTIVITY: Cut ears from felt and glue them onto the upper half of a flat toothpick. Use the mini-marshmallows for legs and tails. Easter grass can be arranged around the bunny to look like grass. Glue in place, then hide different colored jelly beans in the grass to look like Easter eggs. Snack on any leftovers (do not allow young children to eat marshmallows).

CONCEPTS:
- creative thought
- spatial relationship
- size comparison
- color

VARIATIONS: This is a perfect time to learn some Easter songs for Music ("Here Comes Peter Cottontail"...) . Study the rabbit family (and other woodlands animals) and their animal behavior and lifestyle for Science. Have children name famous fictional rabbits from movies and cartoons. Discuss their favorites. Sort colored jelly beans, count and/or graph for a Math project.

MATERIALS: hard boiled eggs
package of Easter egg food dyes
glue
paper or clear plastic eggs from craft store

ACTIVITY: Dye eggs according to package instructions. Peel eggs and crush different colored shells together in a bowl. Use egg shells to glue a design onto the paper. For a different approach, make a kaleidoscope by sprinkling glue into clear plastic eggs and shake the egg shells inside the egg. Let the eggs dry.

   Make a clear egg kaleidoscope without gluing the colored shells. Put the colored shells inside the eggs. Glue the two halves of the plastic egg together so infants cannot get inside. Watch them swirl, shake and examine the colored shells.

   Toddlers will enjoy filling and emptying the egg shells over and over again. Remember to be with them at all times.

CONCEPTS:
- ◆ color recognition
- ◆ spatial relationship
- ◆ fine motor skills

VARIATIONS: As a Science unit, talk about the origin of eggs and encourage children to name animals and birds that lay eggs. Use the leftover hard boiled eggs from the kaleidoscope egg project so the children can make their own egg salad sandwiches for a snack and lesson in Nutrition. Review the food groups and which food group the eggs belong to. Go on a field trip to a farm to watch or help gather eggs.

MATERIALS: balloons
flour/water
string

PREPARATION: Mix flour and water using the papier-mâché recipe shown in Chapter 2. Prepare the work area with newspapers and smocks for kids. Blow up and tie the balloons.

ACTIVITY: Dip the string into the paste and wrap string around balloon until covered (foot long pieces of string are easier for younger children to work with). Allow to dry and pop balloons for an intricate effect. Hang them from the ceiling as decorations.

CONCEPTS:
- hand-eye coordination
- size estimation/ shapes

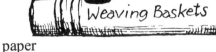

← slide strips over

MATERIALS: paper
1" wide paper strips
scissors/stapler

PREPARATION: Fold paper in half. Cut straight lines every inch, leaving a solid inch at each end.

ACTIVITY: Weave each strip in and out of slots as shown in diagram. Alternate strips for a weaving effect. Trim excess strips even with paper. Staple or glue each end of each strip. Fold opposite corners and staple strip to each corner for a handle. Have children put Easter grass and goodies into their baskets.

CONCEPTS:
- problem-solving
- fine motor skills
- colors/patterns
- hand-eye coordination

PARENTS' DAYS

MATERIALS: empty play dough cans
pretty stickers or paper
scissors/glue/markers
inexpensive flat of 4-8 flowers
potting soil

PREPARATION: Pre-draw about ten small sticker size decorations (ie: rainbows, mushrooms, butterflies, watermelons, apples, flowers, etc.).

ACTIVITY: Children color and cut decorations and glue a pattern onto the outside of the play dough cans. When they are dry, laminate the can with contact paper. Have children make cards to match by drawing the same design on a folded piece of paper. When the pots are complete, let the children plant flowers in them. Moms will love them for Mother's Day.

Precut paper and decorations for older infants and toddlers to glue (guide hands). Help them plant their seeds into the potting soil.

CONCEPTS:
- ◆ fine motor skills
- ◆ creative thought
- ◆ horticultural concepts/life forms

VARIATIONS: Reinforce Science concepts by discussing the parts of the flower and what makes the flower grow. Make a graph of the growing process for a Math activity.

MATERIALS: paper
markers

PREPARATION: Copy and enlarge a USA map outline (if parents are from a different country, refer to a world atlas and trace country outline).

ACTIVITY: Children design little flags from paper and use those flags to mark the birthplaces of their fathers, mothers, grandparents, siblings, and selves. Have them dictate a list of qualities that they like best in each of their family members. Give the maps to parents as a gift for Mother's Day and Father's Day.

 Write stories about each family member. Illustrate and design covers to make books to give away.

CONCEPTS:
- ◆ geographical locations
- ◆ creative thought
- ◆ self-awareness
- ◆ problem-solving

FOURTH OF JULY

MATERIALS: Styrofoam cups
gray/black paint
paint brushes

ACTIVITY: Paint the Styrofoam cups with gray paint. When the cups are dried, paint a crack from the cup opening to resemble the crack in the Liberty Bell, and turn the cups upside down.Visit a travel agent for brochures of Philadelphia. Cut out historical pictures to make a collage. Write a story to accompany the collage.

CONCEPTS:
- ◆ historical significance
- ◆ fine motor skills
- ◆ celebrations

VARIATION: Draw ten small Liberty Bells on paper. Have the children color and cut them out. Use the bells to reinforce counting skills or learn addition and subtraction concepts for Math. Write numbers on each bell and laminate to use in the future for number recognition.

Liberty Silhouettes

MATERIALS: construction paper
(black, red, white, blue)
scissors
white crayon/marker
glue

PREPARATION: Use the white crayon to copy the Statue of Liberty pattern onto black paper. Cut red and blue 2" paper strips.

ACTIVITY: Discuss the significance of the Statue of Liberty in accordance with the Fourth of July celebration. Show the children pictures of the statue from library books. Cut silhouettes from the black paper. Glue red and blue strips onto the white paper to make a patriotic background. Place the silhouette over the background.

 Older infants can pat pre-glued paper strips onto the white paper. Cut their silhouettes.

 Cut out many silhouettes and create a design. Design a special flag using a silhouette. Research the history of the Statue of Liberty (the transportation, creator, installation, and foreign implications).

CONCEPTS:
- ◆ historical significance
- ◆ silhouette
- ◆ color

- contrast
- celebration

During those summer months, vacations and after school times, older children have a tendency to get bored. We can help to keep them stimulated.

MATERIALS: paper
                 markers

PREPARATION: Make up a fun-sheet by tracing a picture of the kid's favorite cartoon character (Ninja Turtles, Snoopy, Winnie the Pooh, Barbie, etc.). Draw the outline of shapes that coincide with the character (ie: bones for Snoopy, balloons for Winnie, fireballs for the Ninja Turtles, etc.) In each shape, write down activities from the list below. While you are working with preschoolers, toddlers and infants, school age children can work on their Activity Challenge Sheets. As each fun activity is completed, the children color the shape. When all the shapes are colored, the sheet is completed, and they can color the cartoon character. Continue making new sheets with new activities throughout the summer or even after school.

ACTIVITIES FOR FUN-SHEET

- 1. Create a new holiday. Include foods, dress, reason for celebrating, traditions, and date.

- 2. Make a relief map of your state using play dough and cardboard. Dry and paint.

- 3. Make up your own board game.

- 4. Carve a bar of soap into anything.

- 5. Build a house with popsicle sticks, milk cartons, shoeboxes, or other cartons.

- 6. Have a scavenger hunt in the want ads of your newspaper (find your favorite job, car, house, entertainment, etc.)

- 7. Pick an unusual animal. Read about it and write an article with illustrations. Read your article to the other children.

- 8. Invent a comic strip character and write your own comic strip.

- 9. Make a list of summer activities and draw pictures.

- 10. Pick a place you would like to visit anywhere in the world. Write a story about a make-believe visit there. Draw imaginary photographs that you may have taken during the visit.

◆ 11. Look up the history of any of the following items. Share the information with the group.

pizza	movie stars	famous people
ice cream	circus	sports figures
popcorn	Eskimos	balloons
kites	Australian	computers
make-up	natives	toys
trains	transportation	

CONCEPTS:

- ◆ independent thinking
- ◆ problem-solving
- ◆ research skills
- ◆ various subject development
- ◆ spelling
- ◆ reading skills
- ◆ presentation

x = activity

COLUMBUS DAY

Sea Adventure

MATERIALS: library books about Columbus
paper
pencil

PREPARATION: Research Columbus' voyage. Read a story to the children about Columbus.

ACTIVITY: Have a group discussion about what it would be like to have sailed with Columbus. Have older children write a list of necessities for a trip. Role-play the action on board ship by making believe the children are sailing with Columbus (infants and toddlers can be the children of pretend adults). Discuss the dangers, problems and possible feelings that may have arisen during the voyage.

Deviled Eggs Ships

MATERIALS: hard boiled eggs
mayonnaise/mustard
toothpicks
paper
glue/scissors

ACTIVITY: Make deviled eggs by slicing hard boiled eggs lengthwise, mixing the yolks with mayonnaise and mustard, and spooning the mixture into the egg white holes. Cut small triangles for ship sails and glue to the toothpicks. When dried, insert sails into the deviled eggs to resemble Columbus' ships (the Nina, Pinta, and Santa Maria). After a discussion about Columbus or after reading a Columbus story, eat the eggs for snack. Check with your doctor before serving eggs to infants.

CONCEPTS:
- ◆ historical significance
- ◆ nutritional values
- ◆ fine motor skills

VARIATION: Use walnut shells for the ships. Line the inside of the shell with playdough or clay and insert toothpick sails into the dough. Nuts should not be eaten by young children. Review food groups to reinforce Nutritional concepts.

Note: This activity has been adapted with permission and courtesy of Wildwood Resources, Inc..

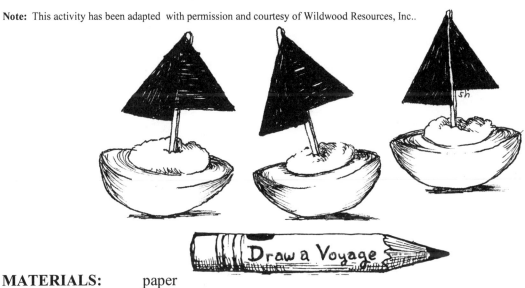

MATERIALS: paper
markers/pencils

PREPARATION: Tell the children that they are going to make believe they are explorers. Explain different ways explorers have traveled (by ship, horseback, foot, spacecraft, wagon train, etc.). Have children draw pictures of the way they would travel if they were explorers.

ACTIVITY: Children create their own maps (real or make believe land and water). Encourage them to think of why they are going exploring (for new land, gold, fountain of youth, cure for cancer, new flavor of ice cream). Decide whether this exploration is taking place in the past, present or future. Design a mode of transportation to be used (or use any from the past and present). Make a list of supplies to take. Draw pictures or write a story about the journey. Encourage children to solve situations that may arise. Complete the map showing the beginning, middle and end of the journey. Share the project with the younger children.

CONCEPTS:

- historical significances
- problem-solving
- creative thought
- language development
- geographical awareness/mapping skills
- role-playing

HALLOWEEN

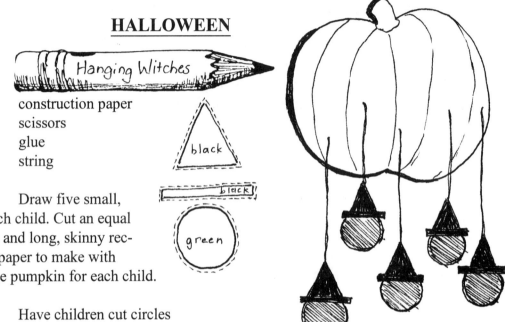

Hanging Witches

MATERIALS: construction paper
scissors
glue
string

PREPARATION: Draw five small, green circles for each child. Cut an equal amount of triangles and long, skinny rectangles from black paper to make with hats. Draw one large pumpkin for each child.

ACTIVITY: Have children cut circles and glue the triangles and rectangles onto the top half of those circles. Cut strings to hang witches from the bottom of the pumpkins to make a mobile.

Make a mobile to hang for infants.
Direct gluing hats onto witches. Have toddlers glue witches onto pumpkins and count.

Have older children design their own witches. See how many different types they can create (fat, really ugly, witches on "new fangled" brooms, witches with cats, witches with cauldrons, etc.). Incorporate witches into a sophisticated mobile. Older preschoolers and kindergartners can participate in this variation.

CONCEPTS:

- shape/color recognition
- fine motor skills
- counting/number recognition
- problem-solving
- creative thinking skills

204

VARIATION: Write a particular number (1-12) on the pumpkin. Make the same amount of witches to hang from the pumpkin to reinforce number recognition and counting skills for Math.

MATERIALS: construction paper (white, brown, orange, blue, black)
glue
razor knife (adults only)

PREPARATION: Cut houses from black paper as shown in the diagram. From brown paper, cut two roofs per house. With the razor blade, cut windows and doors. Fold windows and doors so they open.

ACTIVITY: Glue houses onto blue paper. Be sure the children do not glue the windows or doors. Glue roofs onto the house. On white paper, draw as many ghosts as there are openings and cut out. Tell the children they are going to hide the ghosts in their haunted houses. Glue one ghost under each opening. Count the ghosts and see if they can remember how many and where they are.

Play peek-a-boo together with a finished haunted house.

Cut everything ahead of time (unless your toddler can cut with your help). Direct gluing. Let the children play peek-a-boo or count the ghosts for them. See if they can find all the ghosts.

Write addition, subtraction, multiplication, division, fraction reduction problems, etc. on the ghosts. Write the answers to these problems onto the pumpkins and the children can match the problem with the answer.

CONCEPTS:
- ◆ counting
- ◆ memory development
- ◆ hand-eye coordination
- ◆ number recognition

VARIATIONS: Make spiders and ghosts. On the ghosts, write lower case letters and on the spiders write capitals. Have the children glue all the ghosts inside the house and match the corresponding spiders by gluing them to the correct window or door. For additional Reading and Language variations (depending on the level of each child) match all capitals with all lower cases; use word matches, rhyming words, sounds vs word matching, synonyms and opposites.

HAUNTED HOUSE PATTERN

Chimney

Spire

Roof with Gables

← dummy window w open. Dan cut this one.

Cut all around the windows and door except at the dotted line, which is to be folded (for opening & closing the aperture).

MATERIALS: glue
paper (white and contrasting color)
scissors

PREPARATION: Draw different sized ghosts on two different pieces of white paper.

ACTIVITY: Have children cut all the ghosts from one piece of white paper. Tell the children that they will pick a ghost and match it to one of the ghosts on the uncut paper. Glue the cut out ghosts next to the matching ones.

CONCEPTS:
- ◆ same/different
- ◆ matching
- ◆ fine motor skills

The Changing Pumpkin

MATERIALS: paper
marker
scissors

PREPARATION: Using the pumpkin pattern, draw a pumpkin on construction paper. Write THE CHANGING PUMPKIN poem in the middle of the pumpkin, using a black felt tip marker.

ACTIVITY: Read the poem to the children several times. Act out the poem as you say it together. Children can color and cut out their pumpkins. Follow up with a hands-on activity by choosing a pumpkin, touching it, describing the feel and looks, carving it and lighting the candle inside.

 Set infants on your lap. While reciting the poem hold their hands and make the actions for them.

 Toddlers will love to act out the poem. Guide any cutting or cut their pumpkins for them.

Have older children write their own poem about pumpkins.

CONCEPTS:
- rhyme
- language development
- creative role-playing
- fine motor skills

The Changing Pumpkin

Over there is a pumpkin (point)
That is round as can be. (make a circle in the air)
It is orange and smooth (rub hands together for "smooth")
And is waiting for me. (point to yourself)

I take it right home (act like you're carrying a pumpkin)
And then carve it out, (make believe you're carving)
Clean the white seeds (turn on make believe faucet and wash)
That are lying about. (make sweeping motion with arms)

I cut 'til I give it (make believe you're cutting)
Some eyes and a smile. (point to your eyes and smile)
He looks pretty cut (look cute)
Until after awhile (look at a pretend watch)...

...when the candle is glowing (make a circle with your arms above your head)
And there's darkness outside.
He becomes really spooky (make a spooky face)
So I run fast and hide! (run away and hide).

Denise Theobald

208

MATERIALS: See following list.

PREPARATION: Tell the children they are going to create a spook house in a designated room of the house or school room. Brainstorm with the children for ideas on the spook house. Make a list of responsibilities for each child to volunteer. Here are some ideas to get started.

- **Buy or make scary pictures such as skeletons, ghosts, witches, etc., to hang around the room. Hang rubber spiders, snakes and creepy crawlers from corners and ceiling.**

- **Cobweb material can be purchased reasonably and hung everywhere.**

- **Cut out footprints (be creative and make monster prints or Frankenstein prints). Place footprints on the floor to guide visitors by Halloween decorations and scary areas.**

- **Make feely boxes with "goopy" play dough, grapes, cooked spaghetti, etc.**

- **Have a tape playing with scary sounds.**

 Involve older children as much as possible with the preparation.

ACTIVITY: When the spook house is complete, the children can go through it in pairs. Use a flashlight to follow the footprints. With each new "spook" encountered, ask the children if the prints they are following "belong" to that spook. It's fun and stimulates the imagination.

 If the spook house is more "fun" than "scary", then you may want to let these age groups participate in enjoying the activity, but never force them if they are scared.

CONCEPTS:
- organization skills
- problem-solving
- creative thought

MATERIALS: black felt
empty soap bottle
glue/scissors

green yarn
Styrofoam ball (3" diameter)

PREPARATION: From the felt, cut a large circle double the height of the soap bottle. Cut slits to the middle of the circle and two notches to form a "Y" shape cut. Do the same thing with a smaller circle for the hat. Cut strips of yarn to desired length for the hair.

ACTIVITY: Push the Styrofoam ball onto the tips of the soap bottle until secure. Cover the bottle with the large circle and glue seam shut. Children can then glue strips of yarn to the Styrofoam ball to simulate hair. Make cone shapes from small felt circles for the hats and glue seams. Using straight pins, pin hats to Styrofoam.

 Give infants pieces of felt to touch, Styrofoam balls (supervise to keep balls out of mouths!) to hold, touch, and throw. Describe objects (ie: hat, green, hair, round, head, smooth, rough). Be descriptive.

 Toddlers can be involved with this project. With some guidance, they will help you make their witches.

CONCEPTS:
- ◆ fine motor development
- ◆ shapes
- ◆ colors

VARIATION: Read a storybook with witch characters to prelude this activity (cute stories are better for young listeners).

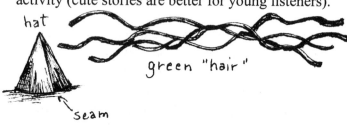

hat

green "hair"

seam

styrofoam ball for head

cut line seam

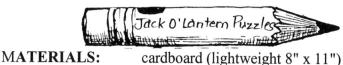

Jack O'Lantern Puzzles

MATERIALS: cardboard (lightweight 8" x 11")
glue/glue brush
black marker
scissors
orange construction paper

PREPARATION: With a black marker, draw pumpkins onto orange construction paper.

ACTIVITY: Children can draw their own faces on their pumpkins to create individual jack-o'-lanterns. With a glue brush and glue, the children can smooth the entire surface of the back of the paper. Carefully matching corners, glue paper onto the cardboard and smooth. For best results, flatten under heavy books before cutting out the puzzle. If desired, laminate the jack-o'-lantern puzzles using the laminating tips in Chapter 2.

 Laminate a whole jack-o'-lantern and let them play with the pieces by bending, mouthing, investigating, etc. Tell your baby all about pumpkins.

Cut toddlers' jack-o'lanterns. Draw faces and cut into simple puzzles.

Have older children draw intricate puzzles and cut more difficult patterns.

CONCEPTS:
- ◆ spatial relationships
- ◆ matching
- ◆ hand-eye coordination
- ◆ problem-solving

All About Pumpkins

toddlers   preschoolers   older

MATERIALS: encyclopedias/library books about pumpkins
                   l pkg. pumpkin seeds
                   l pumpkin

PREPARATION: Read about pumpkins. Locate a pumpkin field near your area.

ACTIVITY: Visit a pumpkin patch with the children. Pick some leaves to take home. Buy the pumpkin that the children have picked out. Show them how the pumpkin grows on the vine. Cut open the pumpkin at home. Let the children touch, smell, and learn each section of a pumpkin (ie: stem, skin, meat, membrane, seeds). Open the packaged seeds and compare the fresh with the prepackaged. Have the children close their eyes and describe the feel, smell, and size. Weigh and measure.

 Both infants and toddlers can be involved. Be sure to include them in your conversations even if they may not understand concepts.

CONCEPTS:
- ◆ vocabulary development
- ◆ growth and discovery
- ◆ sensory development
- ◆ deductive reasoning
- ◆ comparison

VARIATIONS: Children can estimate the number of seeds, then count and graph results for a Math lesson. Follow up the activity by using the pumpkin to bake a pie for Nutrition. Plant the seeds in little cups filled with dirt and record the progress for a Science lesson. Laminate pumpkin leaves into designs for an Arts and Crafts project.

THANKSGIVING

MATERIALS: picture book about Thanksgiving
construction paper (white, black, yellow)
scissors/glue
crayons
popsicle sticks

PREPARATIONS: Copy the Pilgrim and Native American patterns onto white paper. With a white crayon, copy the pilgrim hat pattern onto black paper (big enough to fit a child's head). Make white collars by cutting a circle from the middle of a large rectangular piece of paper. Indian headbands can be made by cutting two 2" x 12" strips of paper and stapling together.

ACTIVITY: After reading a story about the first Thanksgiving, the children can color and cut out their Pilgrim and Native American puppets. Glue a popsicle stick to the back of each. Recreate the first Thanksgiving through the use of the stick puppets.

Next, children cut the hats, collars and headbands. Decorate headbands with feathers (either paper or real), beads, popcorn or other items. Recreate the first Thanksgiving again by dressing up and playacting. Have a discussion about which method of acting the children prefer (through dress-up or puppets) and why.

Allow the children to color the puppets that you have pre-cut. Encourage them to use their puppets in creative ways. Talk about the puppets with the children.

CONCEPTS:
- ◆ historical significance
- ◆ cultural differences
- ◆ fine motor skills
- ◆ creative role-playing
- ◆ problem-solving

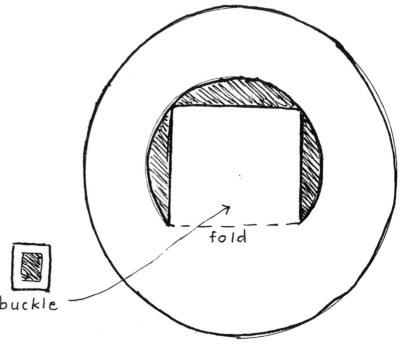

Turkeys Galore

It's always fun to center learning around a theme, especially during the holidays. Here are some quick and fun ideas to create using a turkey theme. All your children can get their hands onto these projects!

MARSHMALLOW TURKEYS

Using toothpicks, large and mini-marshmallows, create turkeys of all sizes and shapes. Cut out beaks, gobblers, wings and eyes from construction paper and stick them into the marshmallows.

PLATE TURKEYS

Use paper plates as the body of a turkey. Cut out a head, neck and feathers to glue onto the plate. Color the turkey with crayons or markers.

PIE TIN TURKEYS

Cut the bottom half side section of a pie tin. Glue paper heads and necks to round bottom of each plate. Hang with string for decoration.

LEAF TURKEYS

Using leaves, build the body of a turkey onto a piece of construction paper. Draw legs, neck, and head to make the leaves into turkeys.

HANDPRINT TURKEYS

Pour a small amount of tempera paint into a flat bowl. Place opened hands flat into the paint. Press print onto paper. Let dry and draw the turkey's feet and other parts.

HANUKKAH

Hanukkah celebrates the purification (Festival of Lights: 165 BCE) of the Temple of Jerusalem. The temple had been desecrated three years earlier when a pagan altar for offering sacrifices to Zeus was established inside the temple. The four symbols shown below are Hebrew symbols representing the phrase "a great miracle happened there." After Judae Maccabee freed Jerusalem from the Greeks, he and his people returned to rededicate the temple. There was only enough oil to light the lamps for a day. The miracle came when the oil continued burning eight days. Hence the significance of eight candles burning in the menorah.

MATERIALS: construction paper
                   scissors/glue

PREPARATION: Draw eight candles and eight flames. On the bottom of a piece of 9" x 12" paper, copy the Hebrew symbols (or allow older children to create them).

ACTIVITY: Have children gather information about Hanukkah: celebrations and traditions. Re-enact these celebrations by using traditional decor, food, etc. Set up a trip to visit a local temple. Children cut out the pictures of candles and flames. On a piece of paper, glue all the candles and count. Then light the candles with the paper flames and count. Math concepts can be reinforced through counting and adding. Write numbers 1 through 8 on the flames and have children sequence them.

CONCEPTS:
- historical significance
- traditions
- counting/ adding
- fine motor skills
- problem-solving

CHRISTMAS

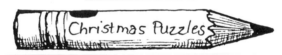

MATERIALS: old Christmas cards
cardboard
rubber cement (or hot glue with supervision)
scissors/razor knives
plastic coating (optional)

ACTIVITY: Glue front of old Christmas cards to cardboard. Trim edges. After drying, cut pictures into puzzles. Play with the puzzles or put puzzle pieces into decorative boxes or inexpensive gift tins to give away.

CONCEPTS:
- problem-solving
- fine motor skills
- traditions (gift giving)

Glitter Jars

MATERIALS: package of inexpensive, miniature ornaments
(ie.: 2" angels, elves, Santa Clauses, etc.)
baby food jars

glitter
waterproof glue

ACTIVITY: Glue waterproof ornaments into the bottom of the baby food jars. Let dry. Fill the jars with water and sprinkle glitter into the jars. Cover with the lid. Shake them up and watch the snow scene. These make great gifts, so wrap them up and give them away!

Reindeer Paws

MATERIALS: construction paper
record or tape player
scissors
tape

PREPARATION: Draw reindeer paw prints on paper. Either pre-cut them or have children cut.

ACTIVITY: Tape paw prints all over the floor. Play Christmas music while the children prance around the room. When the music stops, the children stop of a set of pawprints. Remove a set of prints until there is one winner. If you want the game to be noncompetitive, just repeat the game without removing paw prints.

VARIATION: Use bunny prints for Easter, turkey prints for Thanksgiving and leprechaun prints for St. Patrick's Day. Use this idea as a study of animal prints for Science. Write stories about different prints and adventures of the animals that created the prints for Reading/Language Arts. Count, add, or subtract prints to reinforce Math concepts.

CONCEPTS:
- ◆ fine motor skills
- ◆ creative thinking
- ◆ design

Have a small Christmas tree just for the kids to decorate with homemade ornaments. This builds self-esteem and is fun, too! Here are a few quick ideas and patterns for ornaments:

REINDEER ORNAMENTS

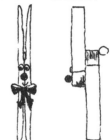

Glue clothespins together, as shown, to form reindeer. Paint clothespins brown. Glue craft eyes, noses, and bows for decoration. Use hot glue to attach string for hanging.

PRETZEL ORNAMENTS

Use different shapes and sizes of pretzels. Glue together to make unique decorations. Decorate individual pretzels with shells, cereal, beans, etc. and shellac (or use a decoupage paste for a glossy shine). Hang with ribbons and strings.

DOUGH ORNAMENTS

Make and roll out homemade dough. Use Christmas cookie cutters (angels, gingerbread boys, stars, etc.) and cut out ornaments. Using a toothpick, make a l/4" hole at the top of the ornament. Place on cookie sheet and bake in a low temperature oven until hardened. After cooling, paint to decorate. When the paint is dried, use a shiny gloss finish to preserve.

FOIL BELLS

Use aluminum foil to shape and mold into bells. Poke holes in the tops and insert a pipe cleaner. Roll a knot in the pipe cleaner inside the bell. Bend the top of the pipe cleaner like a hook so the bells can be hung on the tree.

TOY SOLDIERS

Copy the soldier pattern onto cardboard, construction paper, Styrofoam plates or another desired material. Use your creative abilities to decide what medium to use to decorate (paint, markers, chalk, glitter, etc.). Make a hole in the top of the soldier to insert hanger hooks.

PINE CONE ANGELS

Use the pattern in this chapter to make angel faces out of construction paper. Color, cut and hot glue faces to pine cones. Decorate pine cones with glitter. Make wings with pipe cleaners, material, felt or construction paper. Halos can be made from wire, paper twist, pipe cleaners or other materials. Hot glue a string onto the pine cone for hanging.

COCONUT ORNAMENTS

Crack open coconuts and clean out the meat. Pieces of shell will vary in shapes and sizes. Drill a hole in each piece for hanging. Cut pictures from old Christmas cards and glue inside the shells. Glitter around the pictures to cover edging. Eat the coconut for snack!

SANTA CLAUSES

Make miniature Santa Clauses on small round pieces of cardboard. Glue cotton balls for beards. Decorate craft clothespins to look like long, skinny Old World Santas. Papier mache Santas can be painted and decorated with cotton and other materials. Use Styrofoam balls or oval containers to paint and decorate into Santas. Explore the many materials and types of Santas you can create!

FELT ORNAMENTS

◆ Trace the rocking horse and candy cane patterns onto felt. Design other ornaments to trace onto felt. Cut out felt and use hot glue to put pieces together (make separate pieces out of different colored felt, ie: saddle, eyes, rungs, etc.), or use one color to make a silhouette and have the children decorate with multiple craft materials. Sew string at the top of ornaments for hanging.

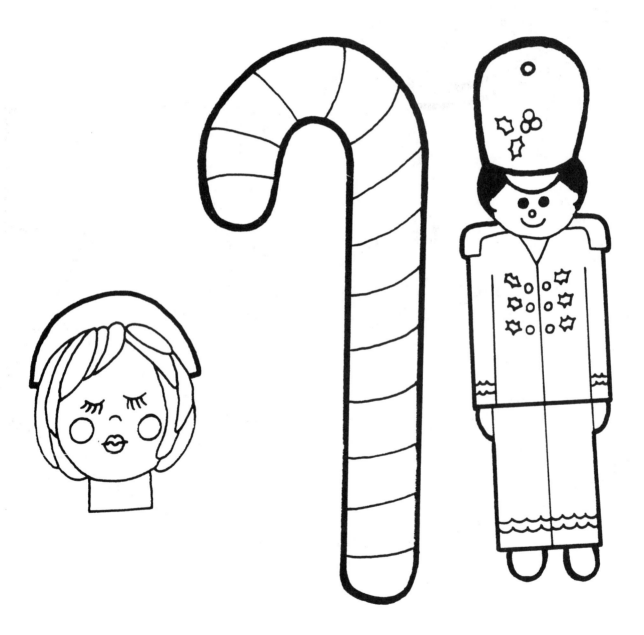

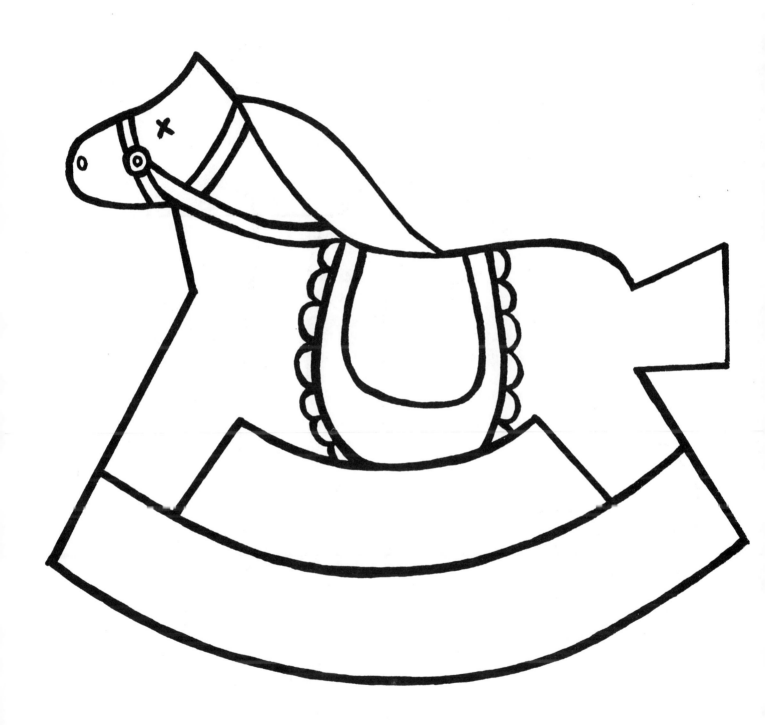

Guides To Computer Programs

READING

- Ready, Set, Read: ages 4-7; Sierra Discovery Series
- Reader Rabbit: ages 3-5; The Learning Company
- Stickybear Preschool: ages 2-6; alphabet, shapes, opposites; Optimum Resource, Inc.
- The Berenstain Bears Learning at Home: Personal and Academic Essentials Your Child Must Know: ages 2-7; multimedia animation, speech, music; Compton's New Media
- Writer Rabbit: grades 2-4; a comprehensive "learning to write" program
- Magic Spells: grades 1-6; spelling program
- Reader Rabbit l: grades K-l; early reading
- Reader Rabbit l: grades l-3; word recognition, spelling, vocbulary skills

READING/WRITING

- Super Print II: grades K-2; publishing, graphics, art
- The Back Street Writer: grades 3-12; word processor
- Talking Text Writer: preschool-6; whole language to develop reading and writing
- Muppet Learning Keys: preschool-l; letters, numbers, counting
- Muppet Word Book: preschool-l; letters, word beginning and endings, mini-word processor
- Muppetville: preschool-l; visual association, shapes, symbols, colors, numbers

MATH

- The Berenstain Bears Learning Essentials: ages 3-9; puzzles, colors, music
- The Playroom: preschool-2; numbers, letters, time, computer skills, counting, playing
- Muppets on Stage: preschool-l; letters, numbers, counting
- Muppetville: preschool-l; visual association, shapes, symbols, colors, numbers
- Math Rabbit: grades K-2; builds early math skills
- Out Numbered: grades 3-5; action adventure that builds math and problem-solving skills
- Math Tutor: grades 1-8; one on one instruction of specific math skills
- Math Shop: grades 1-10; problem-solving skills
- Sidewalk Sneakers: grades K-5; counting, multiples
- Number connections: grades K-3; numbers
- Mountain Monkey Math: grades l-4; computation and problem-solving
- Challenge Math: grades 2-6; whole-numbers and decimals

INTEGRATED STUDIES

- Discrimination, Attributes and Rules: grades K-6; integrated actiavities to build problem-solving skills
- The Berenstain Bears Learning At Home: Personal and Academic Essentials Your Child Must Know: ages 2-7; multimedia animation, speech and music
- Stickybear Preschool: ages 2-6; alphabet, shapes, opposites; Optimum Resource, Inc.
- Spelunx and the Caves of Mr. Seudo: grades K-4; activities in ecology, reading, music, art, astronomy

SCIENCE

- Science Adventure: ages 5+; Isaac Asimov; Interactive Books
- Eco-Saurus: ages 4-9; talking program; First Byte
- Zoo Keeper: ages 6-11; Davidson and Associates, Inc.
- Inner Body Works Jr.: grades 4-6; human body systems
- What's the Difference?: grades 4-6; animal kingdom
- Muppet Labs: grades K-1; science concepts, animals, foundations
- Spelunx and the Caves of Mr. Seudo: grades K-4; activities in ecology, reading, music, art, astronomy

LANGUAGE ARTS

- Just Grandma and Me: preschool-2; Broderbund's Living Books; early reading and storytelling skills
- Arthur's Teacher Trouble: grades K-3; Broderbund's Living Books; early reading and storytelling skills

SOCIAL STUDIES

- Where in the World is Carmen Sandiego?
- Where in America's Past is Carmen Sandiego?
- Where in the USA is Carmen Sandiego?: upper elementary; geography, history, problem-solving skills; Broderbund

MUSIC

- Rock and Bach Studio: ages 7-14; compose, conduct and jam; binary Zoo software
- The Berenstain Bears Learning Essentials: ages 3-9; puzzles, color, music
- The Berenstain Bears Learning at Home: Personal and Academic Essentials Your Child Must Know: ages 2-7; multimedia animation, speech and music
- Spelunx and the Caves of Mr. Seaudo: grades K-4; activities in ecology, reading, music, art and astronomy

Guides For Resource Books

READING

- Saul, Jane, and Sparkman, Brandon. <u>Preparing Your Preschooler for Reading</u>. Schocken Books, 1977 and 1986. This is a book of games introducing reading concepts for preschool children.
- Jett-Simpson, PhD, Mary. <u>Reading Resource Books-Parents and Beginning Reading.</u> Humanics Limited, 1986.
- Freedman Spigman, Robyn. <u>Lollipop, Grapes and Clothespin Critters.</u> Addison-Wesley Publishing, Co. Inc., 1985.
- Kay, Peggy. <u>Games for Reading.</u> Pantheon Books, NY
- Warren, Jean. <u>Teeny, Tiny Folktales</u>. Warren Publishing House, Inc. Everett, WA 98203
- Warren, Jean. <u>Short, Short Stories</u>. Warren Publishing House, Inc., Everett, WA 98203.
- Boynton, Rebecca, and Kobe, Colleen, contributing authors. Compiled by Cromwell, Liz and Faitel, John R., and Hibner, Dixie. <u>Finger Frolics</u>. Gryphon House, 1976. Partner Press, 1983.

SCIENCE

- Brown, Sam Ed. <u>Bubbles, Rainbows and Worms</u>. Gryphon House, Inc., Mount Ranier, Maryland. This book includes science experiments for preschool children.
- Rockwell, Robert E. Sherwood, Elizabeth A., and Williams, Robert A. <u>Mudpies to Magnets</u>. Gryphon House, Inc., Mount Ranier, Maryland. this book is a preschool science curriculum.
- Cassidy, John. <u>Explorabook: A Kid's Science Museum in a Book</u>. The Exploratorium Klutz Press, Palo Alto, CA 1991.
- Walpole, Brenda. <u>175 Science Experiments to Amuse and Amaze Your Friends</u>. Random House, New York, 1988.
- Walpole, Brenda. <u>175 More Science Experiments to Amuse and Amaze Your Friends</u>. Random House, New York, 1989 and 1990.
- Rockwell, Serwood and Williams. <u>Hug a Tree and Other Things to Do Outdoors with Young Children</u>. Gryphon House, Inc., Mount Ranier, Maryland.

INFANTS AND TODDLERS

- Hagstrom, Julie. <u>More Games Babies Play: Fun with Baby from Birth to First Birthday</u>. A + W Visual Library, New York, 1981.
- Buhai Haas, Carolyn. <u>Look at Me</u>. Chicago Review Press, 1987. This book has creative learning activities for babies and toddlers.
- Warren, Jean. <u>Piggy Back Songs for Infants and Toddlers</u>. Warren Publishing House, Inc., Everett, Washington.

MATH

- Collier, Fort and Mac Kenzie. Creative Math Experiences for the Young Child. Incentive Publications, Nashville, Tennessee.
- Kay, Peggy. Games for Math. Pantheon Books, New York. Games are for grades K-3.

INTEGRATED STUDIES

- Collier, Forte and MacKenzie. Kid's Stuff, Kindergarten and Nursery School. Incentive Publications, Nashville, Tennessee.
- Bennett, Steve and Ruth. Kid Pix-Easy Educational and Entertaining Projects for You and Your Child. Random House, l993.
- Warren, Jean. Language Games. Warren Publishing House, Inc. Everett, Washington.
- Forte, Imogen; Mary Ann Pangle; and Robbie Tupa. Pumpkins, Pinwheels and Peppermint Packages. Incentive Publications, Inc. Nashville, Tennessee, l974. This book is full of learning centers and activities for school age children.

CRAFTS

- Fiarotta, Physllis. Sticks and Stones and Ice Cream Cones.
- Better Homes and Gardens. Incredibly Awesome Crafts for Kids. Meredith Corp., Des Moines, Iowa, l992.

NUTRITION

- Klutz Press editors. Kid's Cooking: A Very, Slightly Messy Manual. Illustrated by Guinness, Jim M. Klutz Press, Palo Alto, California, 1987.
- Romaniello RD MS, Catherine Strobl, and Van Domelan, Nancy. Off to a Good Start. Available from Wildwood Resources, Inc., 9085 S. Mineral Circle, Suite 300, Englewood, CO 80112

GAMES AND ACTIVITIES

- Taetszch, Lyn and Sandra Zeitlin. Preschool Games and Activities. Fearon Publishers, Belmont, CA l974.
- Johnson, Anne Akers. Cat's Cradle: A Book of String Fingers. Klutz Presss, Palo Alto, CA, 1993.
- Cassidy, John, and Stillinger, Scott. The Official Koosh Book. Klutz Press, Palo Alto, CA 1989.
- Boyd, Neva L. Handbook of Recreational Games - How to Play More Than 300 Children's Games. Dover Publ., Inc., l985.
- Sackson, Sid and editors of Klutz Press. The Book of Classic Board Games. Klutz Press, Palo Alto, CA John Cassidy, l991.
- Brooke, Maxey. Challenging Coin Games and Puzzles. Dover Publications, Mineola, NY 1991.

NEW PRODUCTS

Teaching Terrific Threes and Other Toddlers

Terry Lynne Graham, M.A.
PAGES: 128 / ISBN: 0-89334-260-2
PRICE: $17.95 / AGES: 3's AND 4's

This long-anticipated sequel to the bestseller *Teaching Terrific Twos* is the ultimate in resource guides for three year olds. Filled with fun and educational activities specifically designed to meet and challenge the abilities and interests of three year olds, *Threes* is a must for anyone involved in caring for this special age group. Activities concentrate on social growth, listening skills, self-image, language skills, fine and gross motor development, and awareness of such concepts as science, math, music, and nutrition. Includes a section about room arrangement, scheduling, discipline, assessment, parent involvement, materials, and basic and individual goals.

Author **TERRY GRAHAM** is one of the most respected authorities on toddlers' education: her insights are a wonderful addition to any child care library.

Bottle Cap Activities: Recycled Crafts for All Ages

Kathy Cisneros
PAGES: 112 / ISBN: 0-89334-279-3
PRICE: $12.95 / AGES: 7 AND UP

From simple to sophisticated crafts, these innovatively creative projects are made of non-recyclable plastic bottlecaps! These free materials, when re-used into ingenious craft projects, are kept out of landfills and thus reduce pollution, which makes them a great lead-in for environmental science lessons- or just for fun! These wonderful ideas are versatile enough for use in classrooms, parties, summer camps, boy and girl scout troops, projects at home, and even senior citizen homes. Also included is the musical play "*The Bottle Cap Kids*" performed at Disney World, with words, sheet music, and instructions for the costume making: even the costumes are made of bottlecaps! Activities include *Bottlecap Barnyard*, *Bottlecap Band*, a calendar of seasonal bottlecap crafts, and a variety of other fun environmental crafts.

While You Are Expecting: Your Own Prenatal Classroom

F. Rene Van DeCarr M.C. & Marc Lehrer, M.D.
PAGES: 160 / ISBN: 0-89334-251-3
PRICE: $16.95

Featured on Oprah, Donahue, The Today Show, ABC Evening Magazine and in *Newsweek*, *Reader's Digest*, *Parenting*, *Harper's Bazaar*, *Baby Talk*, *Doctor*, *Your Health*, *Omni*, *Image* and *U.S.A. Today*, this revolutionary guide introduces exercises which allow both parents to communicate with their unborn baby. Also included are tips for stress reduction and how to provide an optimum prenatal environment for your baby. Easy-to-use, this internationnally recognized manual explains the stages of your baby's physical and mental growth, while concentrating on interactive exercises which result in the easy birth of a calm, intelligent child who has already formed strong, loving, and communicative bonds with his or her parents.

CALL TOLL FREE 1-800-874-8844 • IN GEORGIA (404) 874-2176 • FAX (404) 874-1976 • EMAIL: learning@humanicspub.com